Tales of Twin Cities

A Who's Who Storybook of Nationally renowned persons, both living and dead, who were either native-born, came to reside, or are indelibly identified with Minneapolis and Saint Paul.

Published By

Hornet Publications
Box 10744
Mpls. MN 55440

Copyright 1986

Library of Congress Catalog Card Number: 86-83113

Printed by Anderberg-Lund Printing, Minneapolis

About the Author

Angus Grant was born in Duluth, Minnesota...has resided in Minneapolis since 1937...attended West High School and the University of Minnesota...wrote for The West High Times and Minnesota Daily...Additionally did articles for TV Times, a hockey publication "The Back-Checker", "The Lake Area", The "Green Sheet", and currently publishes the "Metro Hornet". He also wrote a book in 1981 entitled "Minneapolis Memories", and holds a Copyright on "Scottish Clans, Tartans, and Families", an ethnic publication.

About the Artist

Should the exceptional art work herein ring a familiar "memory bell", don't be too surprised.

Mr. Al Papas, Jr. (without whose yeoman efforts this book could not have been completed on schedule) was formerly with The Minneapolis Star and Tribune as was his father Al Papas Sr. Their work bears certain similarities, and Papa Papas was with the newspaper from the early 30's until his untimely death at the age of 44 when Junior took over.

Therefore the odds are that your eyes have feasted on a Papas drawing in the past. We hope you'll view many more in the future.

Acknowledgments

Without the assistance of dedicated Minneapolis Library personnel in helping to locate the material necessary to research the personages, it would have been difficult if not impossible to complete. We are fortunate to have libraries in both Minneapolis and Saint Paul who have spent time and money to maintain the proper materials. We would like to express special thanks to Sally Jungers and Amy Ryan of the Minneapolis History Department for their valuable help.

Index

Preface

What now seems like only yesterday, I was carried away "kicking and screaming" from my early boyhood friends in Duluth to a place called Washington, D.C. Very few things in my memory cells could ever replace many youthful visits to The Smithsonian Institute, The Ford Theatre, the nearby Civil War battlefields, The Senate and The Congress, The Lincoln and Washington monuments, Arlington Cemetery or Griffith Stadium, but when it was time to go back to Minnesota, I was quite ready.

After my father's government stint was completed, we did <u>not</u> return to Duluth, but instead Minneapolis, and <u>still</u> I was happy because it was <u>almost</u> like going back home.

It <u>has</u> been home ever since, for the simple reason that I've traveled just enough to know there isn't a better place in the US of A to reside.

The Upper Midwest's "favorite columnist, Cedric Adams, once ran a contest in which the winner named us "The Theatre of Seasons", and our other dear departed friend, Halsey Hall, whenever someone asked him what he liked about our towns, would exclaim, "Holy Cow", and go on from there to infinity. I could go on and on too, because I've had an ongoing love affair with this area for longer than I care to remember, and it just gets better all the time.

That's why putting this book together was a "labor of love".

Hope you enjoy it.

Historically yours,

Angus Grant

GRANT'S
You Better Believe it!

VETERAN MOTION PICTURE STAR EDDIE ALBERT WAS BORN IN ILLINOIS BUT GREW UP IN MINNEAPOLIS WHERE HE WAS AN ALTAR BOY AT ST. STEPHENS CHURCH. HE WORKED HIS WAY THROUGH THE U OF M BY WASHING DISHES AND USHERING AT A LOCAL THEATER.

EDDIE ALBERT

ALBERT'S REAL NAME WAS HEIMBERGER. WHILE DOING DANCING PERFORMANCES AND RADIO SINGING, ANOUNCERS KEPT CALLING HIM "HAMBURGER" AND SO HE CHANGED HIS NAME TO ALBERT.

THE YOUNG ALBERT WENT TO HOLLYWOOD FROM HIS LOVED BROADWAY. HE HAS DONE MORE THAN 50 FILMS. SOME WERE "ROMAN HOLIDAY" FOR WHICH HE WAS NOMINATED FOR AN OSCAR, AND "OKLAHOMA." YOU MAY ALSO REMEMBER HIM AS THE SADISTIC WARDEN IN THE "LONGEST YARD." MOST OF HIS PARTS, THOUGH, HAVE BEEN AS A GOOD GUY.

HE IS DEDICATED TO THE PROTECTION OF THE ENVIRONMENT AND FEEDING THE POOR THROUGHOUT THE WORLD.

GRANT'S
**You
Better
Believe
it!**

TELEVISION AND MOVIE STAR, LONI ANDERSON, WAS BORN IN ST. PAUL AND ATTENDED ALEXANDER RAMSEY HIGH SCHOOL.

LATER SHE EARNED A B.A. IN ART AT THE U OF M, AND ACTED IN LOCAL THEATRES.

AL PAPAS Jr.

LONI ANDERSON

SHE MOVED TO LOS ANGELES WHERE SHE APPEARED ON "THE BOB NEWHART SHOW," "PHYLLIS," "BARNABY JONES," AND THE "LOVE BOAT." LONI WAS SECOND CHOICE FOR SUZANNE SOMERS PART IN "THREE IS COMPANY," BUT WON HER BEST-KNOWN ROLE AS JENNIFER OF THE "WKRP" CAST.

PLAYING LEAD IN "THE JANE MANSFIELD STORY" SHE RECEIVED GOOD NOTICES WHICH LED TO HER SELECTION BY BURT REYNOLDS FOR THE FEMALE LEAD IN "STAND ON IT."

THE ANDREWS SISTERS

GRANT'S *You Better Believe it!*

FROM NORTH MINNEAPOLIS CAME MAXENE, PATTY AND LAVERNE ANDREOS WHO BECAME THE "QUEENS OF THE JUKE BOX" IN THE 1930's AND 1940's.

THE ANDREOS DANCERS

AL PAPAS Jr.

CHANGING THEIR LAST NAME TO THE ANDREWS SISTERS AND THEIR EARLY DANCE TRAINING TO A SINGING ACT THEY NEARLY ABANDONED THEIR CAREER. THEY WERE DISCOVERED BY DECCA RECORDS ON THE DAY THEY WERE GIVING UP AND GOING HOME TO MINNEAPOLIS. AFTER YEARS OF HARD WORK THIS BREAK MADE THEM A SUCCESS OVERNIGHT WITH "BEI MIR BIST DU SCHOEN."

THEIR FIRST ONE-YEAR CONTRACT WAS FOR $50 PER RECORD, BUT THEY ENDED UP MAKING SUBSTANTIALLY MORE. SOME OTHER HITS WERE "RUM & COCA COLA," "DON'T SIT UNDER THE APPLE TREE" AND "BOOGIE WOOGIE BUGLE BOY." THEIR CAREER SAW THEM SELL OVER 50 MILLION RECORDS.

GRANT'S

You Better Believe it!

JOHN WAYNE, WHO TURNED
DOWN THE PART OF MATT
DILLON ON THE "GUNSMOKE"
TV SERIES, SUGGESTED
JIM ARNESS FOR THE PART.
THE REST IS HISTORY.
AMONG THE WEALTHIEST
OF ACTORS, ARNESS NOW
OWNS ALL THE "GUNSMOKE"
SERIES WHICH WILL BE
AGELESS RE-RUNS.

AL PÄRÄS JR.

JAMES ARNESS (ORIGINALLY
AURNESS) WENT TO WASHBURN
AND WEST HIGH SCHOOLS
IN MINNEAPOLIS. IN JUNIOR
HIGH HE SANG LEAD IN
GILBERT AND SULLIVAN
OPERETTAS. AT WEST
HE WAS AN AVID ENTHU-
SIAST OF ICE-BOATING
ON LAKE CALHOUN.

JAMES ARNESS

WHILE TESTING THE WATER DEPTH WITH HIS 6 FT. 6 IN. FRAME AT ANZIO
BEACHEAD DURING WWII, HE CAUGHT A SNIPER BULLET WHICH CAUSED A
SLIGHT LIMP. HE WAS SENT BACK TO MINNEAPOLIS WHERE HE WAS AN
ANNOUNCER AT WLOL RADIO.

ARNESS LATER HITCH-HIKED TO CALIFORNIA AND ENROLLED IN THE ACTORS
WORKSHOP. THERE A SCOUT RECOMMENDED HIM TO PLAY LORETTA YOUNG'S
BROTHER IN THE ACADEMY AWARD WINNING "FARMERS DAUGHTER" IN 1947.

GRANT'S *You Better Believe it!*

THE SENIOR MOTION PICTURE
STAR OF THE AGELESS CLASSIC,
"ALL QUIET ON THE WESTERN FRONT"
AND THE POPULAR "DR. KILDARE"
SERIES WAS BORN IN MINNEAPOLIS,
AND ATTENDED SCHOOLS LAKE
HARRIET AND WEST. AYRE'S FATHER
WAS A MINNEAPOLIS COURT REPORTER
AND PLAYED THE CELLO IN THE
MINNEAPOLIS SYMPHONY.

AL PAPAS Jr.

Lew Ayres

LEW WAS FORMERLY MARRIED TO ACTRESSES LOLA LANE AND GINGER ROGERS.
IN 1964 HE MARRIED DIANA HALL OF LONDON, ENGLAND.

LEW WORKED HIS WAY THROUGH
THE UNIVERSITY OF ARIZONA
PLAYING GUITAR AND BANJO
FOR CAMPUS DANCES. A
TALENT SCOUT DISCOVERED HIM
PLAYING FOR A BAND IN LOS
ANGELES.

DURING WORLD WAR II AYRES BECAME
A "CONSCIENCIOUS OBJECTOR," BUT OFFERED
HIS SERVICES IN THE ARMY'S MEDICAL
UNIT WHERE HE WAS PRAISED BY HIS
GENERAL AS "AN OUTSTANDING SOLDIER...
I WISH I HAD A BATTALION LIKE HIM."
HE SERVED IN GUINEA, LEYTE AND
LUZON, AND, UNDER HEAVY FIRE PROVED
HIS BRAVERY WHILE ADMINISTERING
TO WOUNDED MEN.

HIS MOVIE CAREER FLOURISHED AFTER
RETURNING TO HOLLYWOOD. MORE
RECENTLY HE HAS APPEARED IN THE TV
REMAKE "OF MICE AND MEN" AND PROGRAMS
"LOVE BOAT," "KNOTS LANDING," AND "LIME
STREET."

GRANT'S
You Better Believe it!

THE FIRST WOMAN TO THE NORTH POLE IS A ST. PAUL NATIVE WHO ATTENDED ST. PAUL ACADEMY, SUMMIT SCHOOL, AND SIBLEY.

AN ADVENTURESOME PERSON, SHE HAS MADE NUMEROUS CANOE, BACKPACK, BIKE, AND CROSS-COUNTRY SKI JOURNEYS.

ANN BANCROFT

IN 1983 SHE REACHED THE TOP OF MOUNT MCKINLEY, IN ALASKA. WHILE ON THE MOUNTAIN HER CLIMBING COMPANION BECAME DELIRIOUS FROM HYPO-THERMIA. SHE SAVED HIS LIFE AND GOT HIM DOWN OUT OF DANGER.

ANN HAS A DEGREE IN PHYSICAL EDUCATION AND IS AN ELEMENTARY SCHOOL TEACHER. SHE IS ALSO A MOUNTAIN CLIMBING, SKI, AND WILDERNESS SKILLS INSTRUCTOR.

ON HER NORTH POLE TREK WITH THE WILL STEGER EXPEDITION IN 1986, HER RESPONSIBILITIES INCLUDED THE EMERGENCY MEDICAL AND VETERIN-ARIAN EQUIPMENT, CINEMATOGRAPHY, PHOTOGRAPHY, AND TRAIL CREW.

You Better Believe it!

KEN BARTHOLOMEW

FROM 1939-1960 THIS SPEED
SKATING GREAT FROM MINNEAPOLIS
REIGNED. HE COMPILED 14 U.S.
NATIONAL, 10 NORTH AMERICAN
AND 4 INTERNATIONAL TITLES.
TO STAY IN SHAPE HE CLIMBED
POLES AS A TELEPHONE REPAIR
MAN.

AT THE AGE OF 54, IN 1974, KEN
CAME OUT OF RETIREMENT TO WIN
A GOLD MEDAL IN THE SENIOR OLYMPICS
AT LAKE PLACID.

NOT THE ONLY ONE IN HIS FAMILY TO BE ABLE TO STAND UP ON SKATES,
HIS BROTHER, EARL, IS IN THE U.S. HOCKEY HALL OF FAME.

AL PAPAS Jr.

GRANT'S You Better Believe it!

THE FOUNDER OF GENERAL MILLS CAME TO MINNEAPOLIS WHEN HE WAS NINE YEARS OLD FROM PHILADELPHIA.

BELL BEGAN LEARNING THE MILLING TRADE AT THE AGE OF TEN AS A LABORER, THEN MILLWRIGHT, CARPENTER, ELECTRICIAN, CLERK, AND EVENTUALLY A BILL COLLECTOR WITH WASHBURN-CROSBY.

HE ATTENDED THE U OF M MAJORING IN CHEMISTRY. AFTER GRADUATING HE CREATED WHAT WAS CONCEDED TO BE THE FIRST LABORIATORY FOR TESTING FLOURS. LATER AS A SALESMAN COVERING MICHIGAN AND INDIANA, HE RETURNED REGULARLY WITH NEW ORDERS AND NEW IDEAS.

IN 1909 HE WAS ELECTED TO THE BOARD OF DIRECTORS, AND LATER BECAME A VICE-PRESIDENT.

JAMES FORD BELL

AFTER BECOMING A KEY NATIONAL FIGURE IN THE FEEDING OF ALLIED NATIONS DURING WORLD WAR I, HE WAS INSTRUMENTAL IN FORMING GENERAL MILLS IN JUNE OF 1928 AND BEING NAMED IT'S PRESIDENT.

SO SOUNDLY HAD HE LAID THE GROUNDWORK FOR THE COMPANY THAT THE 1929 STOCK MARKET CRASH AND ENSUING DEPRESSION BROUGHT A PERIOD OF SOLID GROWTH FOR GENERAL MILLS.

MR. BELL WAS ALSO A DIRECTOR OF AT&T, PULLMAN, AND EASTMAN KODAK. HE DIED IN 1961 LEAVING GENERAL MILLS A WORLD GIANT IN MANY DIVERSIFIED ACTIVITIES.

GRANT'S You Better Believe it!

Patty Berg

MINNEAPOLIS-BORN PATTY BERG LEARNED TO PLAY THE GAME OF GOLF AT INTERLACHEN, ONE OF THE MORE CHALLENGING COURSES IN THE AREA, WHEN JUST A YOUNG GIRL.

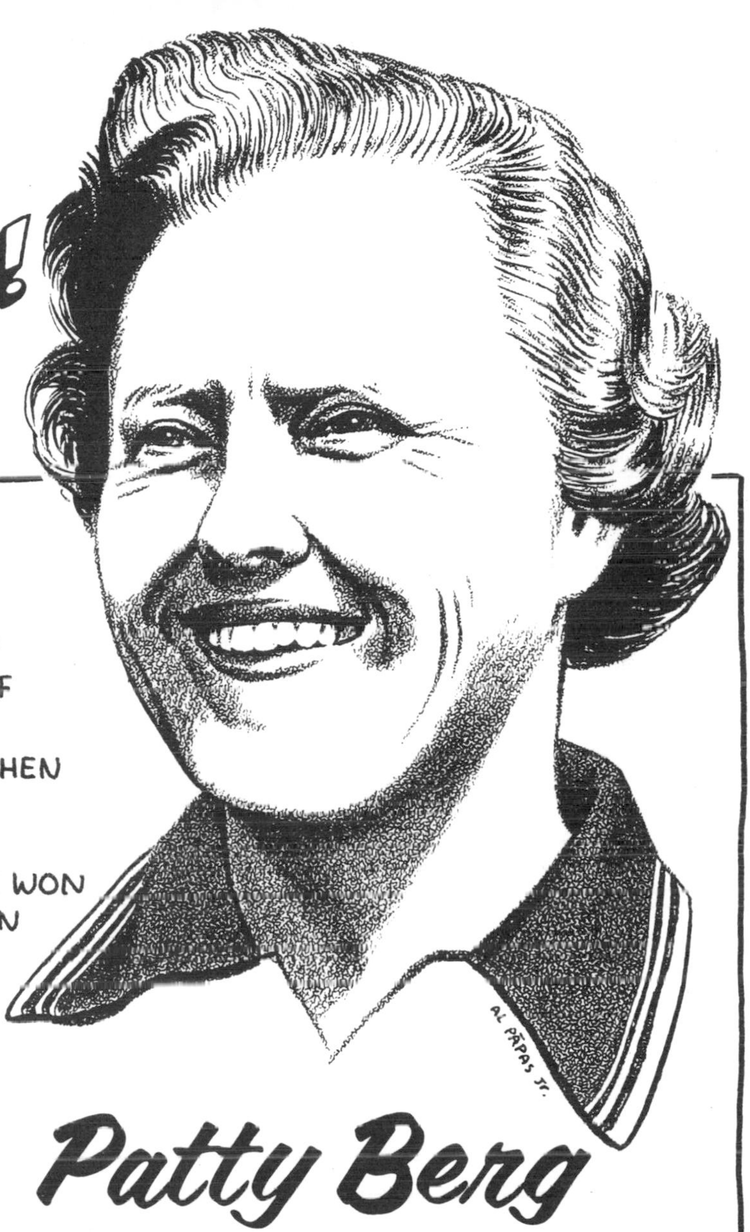

FROM 1934 TO 1940 SHE WON 29 TOURNAMENTS AS AN AMATEUR.

AFTER PLAYING ON TWO CURTIS CUP TEAMS, SHE TURNED PROFESSIONAL AND PROCEEDED TO WIN 55 TOURNAMENTS FROM 1941 TO 1962.

PATTY WAS NAMED ASSOCIATED PRESS "WOMAN OF THE YEAR" DURING THREE DIFFERENT DECADES, 1938, 1943, AND 1955. SHE BECAME A CHARTER INDUCTEE INTO THE WOMEN'S "GOLF HALL OF FAME." SHE IS ALSO THE ONLY WOMAN EVER TO SCORE A "HOLE-IN-ONE" AT A U.S. OPEN.

BERG STILL GIVES CLINICS FOR WILSON SPORTING GOODS. ONCE A YEAR THE LPGA PRESENTS THE "PATTY BERG AWARD" TO THE MAN OR WOMAN WHO HAS MADE AN OUTSTANDING CONTRIBUTION TO THE GAME OF GOLF.

GRANT'S You Better Believe it!

AL PAPAS Jr.

BERNIE BIERMAN 1897-1977

HE WAS NICKNAMED "THE SILVER FOX OF THE NORTHLAND." THE LEGEND-
ARY UNIVERSITY OF MINNESOTA FOOTBALL COACH CAME FROM WASECA
TO MINNEAPOLIS IN 1915.

IN HIS EARLY DAYS AS A PLAYER HE RAN THE 100 YARD DASH IN TEN SEC-
ONDS, AND BECAME CAPTAIN OF THE GOPHER FOOTBALL TEAM.

BIERMAN'S COACHING CAREER SAW HIM AT MONTANA, MISSISSIPPI STATE,
AND TULANE. HE GUIDED TULANE TO THE 1932 ROSE BOWL. AFTER THAT
BOWL GAME HE CAME DIRECTLY BACK TO MINNESOTA TO COACH HIS
ALMAMATER. COACHING FOR 14 YEARS THE GOPHERS BECAME KNOWN
AS THE "GOLDEN GOPHERS" UNDER HIS TUTELAGE.

DURING THE "GOLDEN YEARS" BIERMAN PRODUCED 12 ALL-AMERICANS,
WON SIX BIG TEN TITLES, FIVE NATIONAL CHAMPIONSHIPS, AND WAS
"COACH OF THE YEAR" IN 1941. HE IS ALSO ENSHRINED IN THE NATIONAL
FOOTBALL HALL OF FAME.

GRANT'S You Better Believe it!

THIS MINNEAPOLIS-BORN YALE GRADUATE LATER EARNED A LAW DEGREE FROM THE UNIVERSITY OF MINNESOTA. AFTER ENGAGING IN PRIVATE PRACTICE HE JOINED MINNEAPOLIS HONEYWELL RISING RAPIDLY IN THAT ORGANIZATION TO BECOME IT'S CHIEF EXECUTIVE OFFICER FROM 1964-74. DURING PART OF THE SAME PERIOD HE WAS ALSO A DIRECTOR OF 3M COMPANY FROM 1968-85.

AL PAPAS Jr.

JAMES BINGER

HE IS PRESENTLY INVOLVED TOGETHER WITH HIS WIFE, VIRGINIA, IN THE THEATRICAL AND HORSE RACING BUSINESS. THROUGH THEIR JUJAMCYN THEATRES THEY OWN FIVE OF NEW YORK'S BEST KNOWN, AND ARE OPTING TO ACQUIRE MORE AS THEY BECOME AVAILABLE. THIS COULD MAKE THEM THE LEADER IN THE AMERICAN THEATRE FIELD.

BINGER'S ORIGINAL ENTRY INTO THE THEATRE FIELD WAS AS CHAIRMAN OF THE BOARD OF DIRECTORS OF THE GUTHRIE THEATRE OF WHICH HE IS STILL A BOARD MEMBER.

THE BINGER'S TARTAN FARMS OF OCALA, FLORIDA IS KNOWN AS ONE OF THE FINEST STABLES IN THE UNITED STATES. THOSE IN THE KNOW FEEL IT IS JUST A MATTER OF TIME BEFORE ONE OF THEIR ENTRIES WINS A KENTUCKY DERBY.

GRANT'S You Better Believe it!

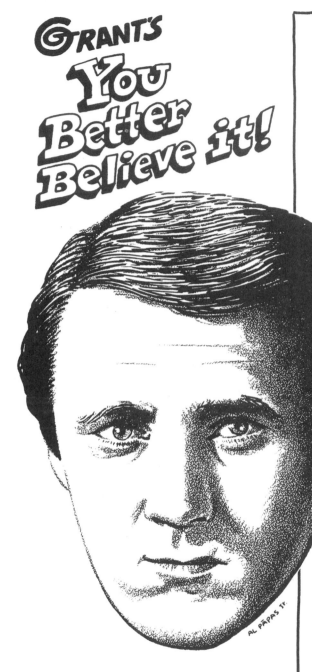

AL PAPAS Jr.

THE MOMENT HE WILL BE FOREVER REMEMBERED FOR WAS HIS GLORIOUS TRIUMPH AT DIRECTING THE U.S. GOLD MEDAL TEAM IN THE 1980 OLYMPICS. IN 10 MONTHS HE TOOK A YOUNG TEAM AND HAD THEM PLAY PRO AND INTERNATIONAL OPPONENTS TO PREPARE THEM TO BEAT THE BEST "AMATEUR" TEAMS IN THE WORLD.

BORN IN ST. PAUL, HERB BROOKS PLAYED HIS EARLY HOCKEY FOR JOHNSON HIGH SCHOOL.

Herb Brooks

IN 1960 HE WAS THE LAST TO BE CUT FROM THE OLYMPIC TEAM THAT WENT ON TO WIN THE GOLD MEDAL AT SQUAW VALLEY. UNDAUNTED HE CONTINUED ON TO PLAY FOR THE GOPHERS AND OLYMPIC TEAMS OF 1964 + 1968 AS WELL AS FIVE U.S. NATIONALS TEAMS.

BROOKS HAD PLANNED TO GO INTO THE INSURANCE BUSINESS WHEN HE WAS ATTRACTED TO BE HEAD HOCKEY COACH AT THE U OF M. WHILE THERE HE GUIDED THE GOPHERS TO NATIONAL CHAMPIONSHIPS IN 1974, 1976, AND 1979.

HE WENT ON TO COACH THE NEW YORK RANGERS AND IS PRESENTLY WORKING ON A NEW HOCKEY DYNASTY AT ST. CLOUD STATE UNIVERSITY.

ALL YOU NEED ARE SOME GOALS!

BROOKS GRADUATED FROM THE U OF M IN 1962 WITH A DEGREE IN PSYCHOLOGY. NO DOUBT IT HAS HELPED IN HIS COACHING.

GRANT'S *You Better Believe it!*

RECENTLY RETIRED CHIEF JUSTICE OF THE UNITED STATES SUPREME COURT, WARREN E. BURGER, WAS BORN IN ST. PAUL.

HE ATTENDED JOHNSON HIGH SCHOOL WHERE HE TOOK PART IN FOOTBALL, HOCKEY, TRACK, AND SWIMMING. DURING SUMMER VACATIONS HE WORKED ON A FARM NEAR RED WING.

HE ENTERED THE U of M, BUT LATER WENT TO WILLIAM MITCHELL COLLEGE WHERE HE GRADUATED MAGNA CUM LAUDE.

Chief Justice Warren E. Burger

HE IS A STAUNCH ADVOCATE OF PRISON REFORM, AND HAS ALSO LASHED OUT PUBLICLY AT SOME ATTORNEYS WHO ARE GUILTY OF "FEE CHURNING," AND PROLONGING CERTAIN CASES. "LAWYERS HAVE A DUTY TO GAIN RESPECT RATHER THAN DISDAIN FROM THE PUBLIC."

BURGER IS A WINE CONNOISSEUR IN ADDITION TO HAVING HOBBIES AT SCULPTING AND PAINTING. HE HAS BEEN HONORED AS A TRUSTEE OF SEVERAL UNIVERSITIES IN ADDITION TO WILLIAM MITCHELL.

PRESENTLY HE IS OVERSEEING THE CELEBRATION OF THE 1987 BICENTENNIAL OF THE CONSTITUTION.

GRANT'S
You Better Believe it!

MINNEAPOLIS BORN SWEDISH-AMERICAN...

Curt Carlson

... IS NOW LEADING THE LIST OF THE WEALTHIEST MINNESOTANS AT $550,000,000. HE IS SOLE OWNER OF THE CARLSON COMPANIES, AN INTERNATIONAL BUSINESS CONGLOMERATE WHICH INCLUDES 75 DIFFERENT COMPANIES EMPLOYING MORE THAN 50,000 PEOPLE. THIS ENCOMPASSES 185 RADISSON HOTELS, RESTAURANT CHAINS AND TRAVEL GROUPS.

WHEN NINE YEARS OLD HE WAS CADDYING AND CARRYING THREE NEWSPAPER ROUTES. HE PAID HIS OWN WAY THROUGH SCHOOL DRIVING A POP TRUCK AND SELLING ADVERTISING. AS A $110 A MONTH SOAP SALESMAN HE BECAME ACQUAINTED WITH THE COUPON REDEMPTION BUSINESS AND BEGAN THE GOLD BOND STAMP COMPANY. THIS WAS THE SPRINGBOARD FOR ALL HIS PRESENT-DAY ACTIVITIES.

CARLSON HAS CONTRIBUTED PERSONALLY $25,000,000 TO THE U OF M AND SPEARHEADED THE RAISING OF ANOTHER $300,000,000. HE HAS RECEIVED INNUMERABLE AWARDS FROM OTHER GOVERNMENTS AND ORGANIZATIONS IN ADDITION TO SERVING ON THE BOARD OF DIRECTORS OF MANY LARGE CORPORATIONS. HE IS CONSIDERED A REAL LIVE "HORATIO ALGER" AND ONE OF THE ULTIMATE ENTREPENEURS IN THE FREE WORLD.

A MINNEAPOLIS WOMAN, BUT
NEVER A REAL PERSON...

Betty Crocker®

...WAS CREATED IN 1921 TO
RESPOND TO HOMEMAKERS BAKING
PROBLEMS AND RECIPE REQUESTS.

THE WASHBURN CROSBY CO., LATER
TO BE GENERAL MILLS, PUT HER ON
THE RADIO "COOKING SCHOOL OF
THE AIR." THE SHOW WON NATIONAL
SUCCESS AND LASTED 24 YEARS.
SHE RECEIVED 4000 CONSUMER
LETTERS PER DAY.

IN 1936 NEYSA McMEIN PAINTED
THE FIRST OFFICIAL PORTRAIT OF
HER (ABOVE). IT WAS DONE FROM A
COMPOSITE OF THE BETTY CROCKER
SERVICE DEPT. EMPLOYEES.

IN 1940 A SURVEY FOUND THAT 9 OUT OF 10
HOMEMAKERS KNEW WHO BETTY CROCKER
WAS. SHE WAS SECOND ONLY TO ELEANOR
ROOSEVELT AS ONE OF AMERICA'S BEST KNOWN
WOMEN.

SIX MORE PORTRAITS OF HER HAVE EVOLVED OVER THE YEARS
WITH HARRIET PERTCHIK CREATING THE LATEST (RIGHT).

AL PAPAS JR.

Grant's You Better Believe it!

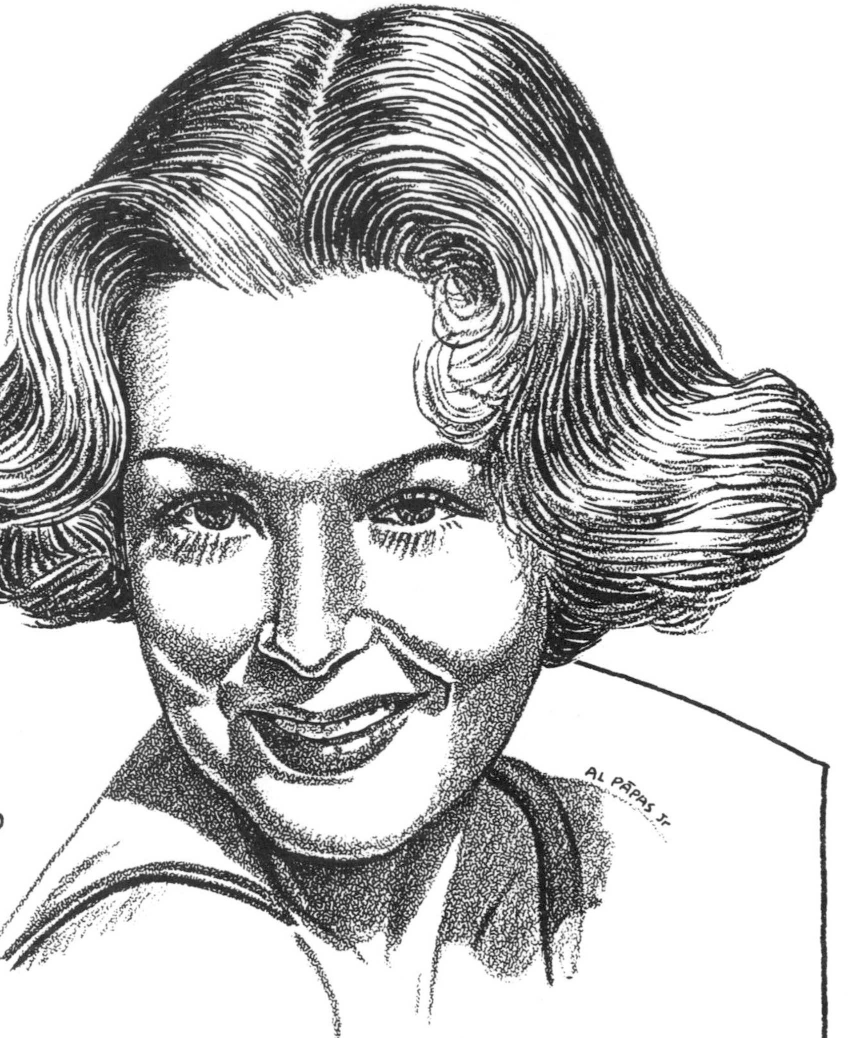

ARLENE DAHL, ONCE REFERRED TO AS THE "MOST GORGEOUS REDHEAD IN THE FILM INDUSTRY," GRADUATED FROM MINNEAPOLIS WASHBURN WHERE SHE WAS NAMED "GIRL MOST LIKELY TO SUCCEED."

Arlene Dahl

SHE STUDIED DRAMA AT THE U OF M BEFORE GOING TO NEW YORK TO MODEL, SING AND ACT. HER FIRST SCREEN TEST RESULTED IN HER SIGNING FOR THE LEAD IN WARNER BROTHERS "MY WILD IRISH ROSE" OPPOSITE DENNIS MORGAN. SHE NEXT APPEARED IN "THREE LITTLE WORDS" WITH A SINGING PART.

ARLENE ALSO DID BROADWAY PLAYS, AUTHORED A BOOK, AND WROTE A NEWSPAPER COLUMN. SHE ALSO DESIGNED HER OWN LINE OF LINGERIE, AND BOUDOIR CAPS BEFORE RISING TO VICE PRESIDENT OF AN AD AGENCY ON MADISON AVENUE.

GRANT'S
You Better Believe it!

GEORGE DRAPER DAYTON WAS BORN IN GENEVA, NEW YORK.

HE CAME TO MINNESOTA IN 1883, LOCATING IN WORTHINGTON. AFTER A SUCCESSFULL BANKING AND CIVIC CAREER IN THAT CITY FOR NINE YEARS, HE ELECTED TO GO TO MINNEAPOLIS AFTER CONSIDERING FIVE OTHER CITIES FOR HIS FUTURE BUS-INESS ENTERPRISE.

HE PURCHASED SEVERAL TRACTS OF LAND ON NICOLLET AVENUE, AND SOON BECAME A RECOG-NIZED LEADER IN THE OWNER-SHIP AND DEVELOPMENT OF MINNEAPOLIS BUSINESS PROP-ERTY.

AL PAPAS Jr.

GEORGE D. DAYTON
1857-1938

IN 1902 HE BOUGHT THE OLD WESTMINISTER CHURCH PROPERTY ON 7TH AND NICOLLET AND ERECTED A SIX STORY BUILDING. AT ABOUT THE SAME TIME HE PURCHASED THE GOODFELLOW DRY GOODS BUSINESS ON LOWER NICOLLET, AND MOVED IT TO HIS 7TH AND NICOLLET SITE.

IN 1903 THE NAME WAS CHANGED TO DAYTON DRY GOODS, AND LATER TO THE DAYTON COMPANY. THAT WAS THE BEGINNING OF WHAT IS TODAY ONE OF THE LARGEST RETAILERS IN THE UNITED STATES ENCOMPASSING DAYTON-HUDSON, TARGET, AND OTHER SUBSIDIARIES.

A LONG SUCCESSION OF DAYTONS HAVE FOLLOWED IN HIS FOOTSTEPS. THE FIRM HAS BEEN ONE OF THE LARGEST CONTRIBUTORS TO THE GROWTH OF THE TWIN CITIES AREA, BUT IT WAS G.D. DAYTON'S EXCEPTIONAL FORESIGHT THAT LAID THE GROUNDWORK.

GRANT'S You Better Believe it!

THIS FAMOUS NOVELIST WAS BORN AT 481 LAUREL IN ST. PAUL. HE WAS NAMED AFTER AN ANCESTOR, FRANCIS SCOTT KEY, WHO WAS THE AUTHOR OF THE "STAR SPANGLED BANNER."

AFTER ATTENDING PRINCETON UNIVERSITY AND SERVING IN THE ARMY HE RETURNED TO HIS PARENTS ROWHOUSE AT 599 SUMMIT AVENUE WHERE HE FINISHED HIS FIRST NOVEL "THIS SIDE OF PARADISE." LEAVING AGAIN TO MARRY A SOUTHERN BELLE, ZELDA SAYRE, HE LATER CAME BACK WITH HIS PREGNANT WIFE TO WORK ON HIS SECOND BOOK "THE BEAUTIFUL AND THE DAMNED."

F. Scott Fitzgerald

1896-1940

AFTER THE FITZGERALDS JOINED THE WHITE BEAR YACHT CLUB AND THE ST. PAUL SOCIETY SWIRL, HE FINISHED SEVERAL SHORT STORIES AND BEGAN THREE MORE BOOKS, "THE GREAT GATSBY," "TENDER IS THE NIGHT," AND "THE LAST TYCOON," WHICH HE NEVER COMPLETELY FINISHED.

HE LATER MOVED TO CALIFORNIA TO BECOME A SCREEN WRITER, BUT DIED AT THE YOUNG AGE OF 44 FROM ACUTE ALCOHOLISM.

MINNEAPOLIS BORN ORVILLE FREEMAN ATTENDED CENTRAL HIGH SCHOOL. LATER, AT THE UofM, HE PLAYED QUARTERBACK UNDER BERNIE BIERMAN AND ATTENDED LAW SCHOOL.

IN 1948 HE HELPED HUBERT HUMPHREY REORGANIZE THE MINNESOTA DEMOCRATIC PARTY. IN 1954 HE WAS ELECTED GOVERNOR OF MINNESOTA AND SERVED THREE TERMS.

Orville Freeman

WHILE SECRETARY OF AGRICULTURE UNDER JOHN F. KENNEDY HE SAT IN THE CABINET DURING THE "CUBAN MISSILE CRISIS" AND MANY OTHER IMPORTANT MEETINGS. HE CONTINUED UNDER THE JOHNSON ADMINISTRATION IN THE SAME POST. LATER HE BECAME CHAIRMAN OF THE BOARD OF BUSINESS INTERNATIONAL CORPORATION IN NEW YORK, AN EXPORT FIRM.

FREEMAN ADVANCED A PLAN TO SAVE CERTAIN PARTS OF THE WORLD FROM STARVATION. THIS RESULTED IN WINNING A $30,000 FIRST PRIZE, IN 1982, AT THE WOODLANDS CONFERENCE ON SUSTENANCE SOCIETIES.

PRESENTLY HIS SON, MICHAEL, IS A STATE SENATOR FROM BLOOMINGTON AND ORVILLE IS NOW ASSOCIATED WITH THE WASHINGTON OFFICE OF A MINNEAPOLIS LAW FIRM.

GRANT'S You Better Believe it!

VERN GAGNE'S INITIAL FAME WAS AS A FOOTBALL PLAYER OUT OF ROBBINSDALE. HE MADE THE U OF M SQUAD AS A FRESHMAN IN 1943. END AND HALFBACK WERE HIS POSITIONS. HE MADE THE ALL-CONFERENCE TEAM AND HONORABLE MENTION IN THE ALL-AMERICAN VOTING. AFTER PLAYING IN THE ALL-STAR GAME OF 1949 HE WENT PRO FOR THE GREEN BAY PACKERS.

AS FAR AS WRESTLING IS CONCERNED, HE WAS STATE CHAMPION IN HIGH SCHOOL AND IN COLLEGE WAS FOUR TIMES BIG TEN CHAMPION. HE ALSO TOOK ONE A.A.U. AND TWO N.C.A.A. CHAMPIONSHIPS AS WELL AS BEING A MEMBER OF THE 1948 OLYMPIC TEAM.

VERN GAGNE

IN 1959 VERN WON THE ULTIMATE IN PROFESSIONAL WRESTLING, THE WORLD'S HEAVYWEIGHT CHAMPIONSHIP. AFTER WINNING AND LOSING THE TITLE A NUMBER OF TIMES HE RETIRED AS CHAMP IN 1981. HE HAS HELD ALL THE CHAMPIONSHIPS AND AWARDS IN HIS BUSINESS WHILE ALSO BEING INDUCTED INTO THE WRESTLING HALL OF FAME IN 1971.

HAVING COME OUT OF RETIREMENT ON OCCASION HE HAS TEAMED UP WITH HIS SON GREG. THERE ARE 50 OR MORE YOUNG WRESTLERS ACTIVE IN THE RING TODAY HE HAS TRAINED.

REPRESENTING WRESTLING, GAGNE HAS APPEARED ON MANY LEADING TALK SHOWS WITH PHIL DONAHUE, MERV GRIFFIN, AND ON PM MAGAZINE, THE TONIGHT SHOW, AND OTHER NETWORK PROGRAMS.

GRANT'S You Better Believe it!

THE WORLD RENOWNED BILLIONAIRE, AND ONE OF THE WORLD'S RICHEST MEN WHEN HE DIED IN 1976...

J. PAUL GETTY

... SPENT HIS BOYHOOD YEARS IN MINNEAPOLIS. HE WENT TO EMERSON GRADE SCHOOL AND LIVED ACROSS THE STREET FROM LORING PARK.

HIS MOTHER HAD HIM TAKE PIANO LESSONS WHILE HIS FATHER GOT HIM INTO BOXING AND WEIGHT LIFTING. GETTY USED TO RECALL HITCHING A RIDE ON HIS SLED TO THE TOP OF HENNEPIN VIA THE HORSE DRAWN TROLLEYS, AND THEN SLIDING BACK DOWN THE HILL.

HIS FATHER BECAME WEALTHY IN THE OIL BUSINESS BUT COULDN'T CONVINCE PAUL TO JOIN HIM. THE YOUNGER GETTY WANTED TO JOIN THE U.S. DIPLO-MATIC SERVICE. LATER HE CHANGED HIS MIND AND EARNED HIS FIRST MILLION BY AGE 23 ... THEN RETIRED. HE CHANGED HIS MIND ABOUT RETIREMENT, TOO.

GRANT'S
You Better Believe it!

HE WAS KNOWN AS "THE PHANTOM" IN NATIONAL BOXING CIRCLES. HE NEVER WON A TITLE BUT WAS KNOWN COAST TO COAST AS THE MAN THE TOP THREE IN HIS DIVISION AVOIDED HAVING TO FIGHT.

GIBBONS WAS RESPONSIBLE FOR MAKING ST. PAUL "THE BOXING CAPITAL OF THE UNITED STATES" IN THE EARLY "TEENS."

AS AN OUTSTANDING RING INNOVATOR, HE WAS TABBED AS THE GREATEST DEFENSIVE FIGHTER OF HIS ERA. HE LOST ONLY THREE FIGHTS DURING HIS ENTIRE CAREER.

Mike Gibbons
1889 – 1958

AFTER HIS RING DAYS HE WROTE A BOOK ENTITLED "HOW TO BOX AND HOW TO TRAIN." IT WAS A WORLDWIDE SELLER BECOMING A STANDARD IN PUBLIC AND SCHOOL LIBRARIES.

IN 1931 GIBBONS RAN FOR, AND WAS ELECTED ST. PAUL'S CITY CLERK FROM A FIELD OF THIRTEEN. AFTER THAT HE BECAME A SUCCESSFUL INSURANCE AGENT UNTIL THE TIME OF HIS DEATH.

GRANT'S You Better Believe it!

BUD GRANT PLAYED FOOTBALL, BASKETBALL, AND PITCHED AMERICAN LEGION BASEBALL IN HIS HOME TOWN OF SUPERIOR, WISC.

COMING TO THE U of M IN 1946 HE WENT ON TO WIN NINE VARSITY LETTERS, AND WAS AN ALL-BIG TEN END IN FOOTBALL. HE WAS VOTED MINNESOTA'S "ATHLETE OF THE HALF-CENTURY" BY A PANEL OF SPORTSWRITERS AND SPORTSCASTERS.

IN 1949 HE WAS SIGNED BY MAX WINTER, WHO WAS THEN PRES-IDENT OF THE MINNEAPOLIS LAKERS, TO PLAY IN THE NBA. HE PLAYED ON TWO OF THEIR CHAMPIONSHIP TEAMS.

BUD THEN JOINED THE PHILA-DELPHIA EAGLES OF THE NATION-AL FOOTBALL LEAGUE WHEN THEY DRAFTED HIM NUMBER ONE. HE WAS THE SECOND RANKING RECEIVER IN THE NFL IN 1952 WITH 57 CATCHES. IN 1953 HE JUMPED TO PLAY IN THE CANADIAN FOOTBALL LEAGUE. IN 1957 HE WAS MADE COACH AT WINNIPEG. WHILE THERE HE WON SIX DIVISION AND FOUR GREY CUP CHAMPIONSHIPS.

BUD GRANT

IN 1967 HE WAS OFFERED THE MINNESOTA VIKINGS JOB. IT WAS TO COVER AN 18 YEAR SPAN DURING WHICH HIS TEAMS HAD A 158-96-5 RECORD, MAKING 12 PLAYOFFS AND WINNING 15 CHAMPIONSHIPS. ALTHOUGH GETTING TO FOUR SUPERBOWLS, HE CAME AWAY WINLESS IN THAT AREA. GRANT IS SECOND ONLY TO THE LEGENDARY GEORGE HALAS IN TOTAL VICTORIES.

AFTER RETIRING A SECOND TIME IN 1985, HE IS NOW ENJOYING HIS FAVOR-ITE PASTIMES OF HUNTING AND FISHING.

GRANT'S
You Better Believe It!

THIS STAR OF MOTION PICTURES AND TELEVISION IS A MINNEAPOLIS AREA RESIDENT WHO GRADUATED FROM SOUTHWEST HIGH SCHOOL IN 1944.

AFTER GRADUATION FROM THE U OF M PETE TOOK HIS MATERNAL GRANDMOTHER'S NAME IN 1949. THIS WAS TO AVOID ANY CONFLICT WITH HIS OLDER BROTHER JAMES ARNESS, OF "GUNSMOKE" FAME, WHO HAD AT THAT TIME MADE SEVERAL MOTION PICTURES.

PETER GRAVES

DURING HIS FIRST YEAR IN THE MOVIE CITY HE WORKED AS A SALESMAN, WAITER, AND CAB DRIVER BEFORE LANDING A ROLE IN "ROGUE RIVER," AND "STALAG 17." LATER HE STARRED IN THE "FURY" AND "WHIPLASH" T.V. SERIES. HIS BIG BREAK CAME AS A LEADER OF THE "MISSION IMPOSSIBLE" GROUP.

WHILE AT SOUTHWEST PETE WAS AN OUTSTANDING HIGH HURDLES TRACK STAR, SETTING RECORDS THAT STILL STAND. HIS CLARINET WAS CONSIDERED "BEST IN THE SOUTHWEST" AND PERFORMED AT MANY LOCAL DANCES. HE STUDIED DRAMA AT THE U OF M AND STARRED IN PERFORMANCES THERE WITH DAVE MOORE WCCO NEWSMAN.

AL PAPAS Jr.

"HAL" GREENWOOD, JR. GREW UP IN MINNEAPOLIS WHERE HE WENT TO SOUTHWEST HIGH SCHOOL.

A NATIONALLY KNOWN FINANCIER, HE IS PRESIDENT AND CHAIRMAN OF THE BOARD OF MIDWEST FEDERAL SAVINGS AND LOAN, WHOSE OVER THREE BILLION DOLLARS IN ASSETS RANKS IT AS ONE OF THE MOST PROFITABLE IN THE COUNTRY. IN ADDITION TO MIDWEST, THERE ARE TWO WHOLLY OWNED SUBSIDIARIES, UNITED MORTGAGE AND GREAT OAK INSURANCE, AND A THIRD, GREENTREE ACCEPTANCE, 20% OWNED BY MIDWEST, AND THE REST BY PUBLIC STOCKHOLDERS.

HAROLD GREENWOOD, Jr.

IN THE EARLY 80'S, DURING A TIME OF EXTREME HARDSHIP FOR MANY S AND L'S, GREENWOOD, AS LEGISLATIVE CHAIRMAN OF THE SAVINGS AND LOAN INDUSTRY, SPENT CONSIDERABLE TIME IN WASHINGTON LOBBYING SUCCESSFULLY ON BEHALF OF THAT GROUP.

GREENWOOD WAS ELECTED PRESIDENT OF THE NATIONAL SAVINGS LEAGUE, AND IS ALSO AN ADVISER TO THE FEDERAL RESERVE BOARD.

AS A LONG TIME SUPPORTER AND ADMIRER OF HUBERT HUMPHREY, THERE ARE MANY WHO FEEL THAT HAD HUMPHREY WON THE SQUEAKY-CLOSE PRESIDENTIAL ELECTION IN 1968, GREENWOOD WOULD HAVE BECOME THE FIRST MINNESOTAN TO BE SECRETARY OF THE TREASURY.

GRANT'S You Better Believe it!

CALVIN GRIFFITH WAS BORN IN CANADA. HE WAS ADOPTED AT AN EARLY AGE BY HIS UNCLE, BASEBALL'S LEGENDARY CLARK GRIFFITH, WHEN HIS FATHER DIED.

UNCLE CLARK, WHO WAS OWNER OF THE WASHINGTON SENATORS, EXPOSED YOUNG CALVIN TO ALL PHASES OF THE GAME, INCLUDING MANAGING ONE OF THEIR MINOR LEAGUE TEAMS.

WHEN CLARK DIED, CALVIN TOOK OVER THE RUNNING OF THE TEAM "STRUGGLING" TO KEEP THE FRANCHISE FINANCIALLY ALIVE WITH THE LEAGUE'S MINIMAL ATTENDANCE NUMBERS.

CALVIN GRIFFITH

WHEN A MINNEAPOLIS GROUP MADE A STRONG PRESENTATION TO HIM IN 1960, HE WISELY ELECTED TO MOVE THE FRANCHISE TO THE TWIN CITIES. DURING 23 YEARS OF OPERATION HE DIRECTED THE MINNESOTA TWINS THROUGH MANY "UPS AND DOWNS," BUT ALWAYS MANAGED TO KEEP THE TWINS FOREMOST IN THE MEDIA.

WHEN BANKER CARL POHLAD MADE HIM "AN OFFER HE COULDN'T REFUSE" FOR THE TEAM, HE ACCEPTED, BUT IS STILL A "CONSULTANT."

GRANT'S You Better Believe it!

AL PAPAS Jr.

DETROIT-BORN...

JUDITH GUEST

... HAS RESIDED IN
THE TWINS FOR A
NUMBER OF YEARS.
CURRENTLY SHE IS
TEACHING CREATIVE
WRITING AT "THE LOFT"
IN MINNEAPOLIS.

IN 1976, HER FIRST NOVEL, "ORDINARY PEOPLE," AFTER BEING
PUBLISHED IN 17 COUNTRIES WAS MADE INTO A MOTION PIC-
TURE BY ROBERT REDFORD. IT RECEIVED THE OSCAR FOR THE
BEST PICTURE OF 1980.

GUEST'S SECOND NOVEL "SECOND HEAVEN" WAS PUBLISHED
IN 1982. SHE HAS ALSO WRITTEN TWO SCREENPLAYS, ONE CALLED
"RACHEL RIVER" AND ANOTHER WHICH IS AN ADAPTATION OF
THREE SHORT STORIES BY ANOTHER AUTHOR. "RACHEL RIVER"
IS CURRENTLY BEING FILMED IN NORTHERN MINNESOTA.

GRANT'S **You Better Believe it!**

John B. Hawley, Jr.

BORN IN FORT WORTH TEXAS, JOHN B. HAWLEY, JR. CAME TO MINNEAPOLIS IN 1924 WITH SOME OF THE PATENTS HE HAD OBTAINED AFTER GRADUATING FIVE MONTHS AHEAD OF HIS CLASS AT CORNELL. THESE ENGINEERING ADVANCES WERE INSTRUMENTAL IN ESTABLISHING NORTHERN PUMP AND NORTHERN ORDNANCE AS THE U.S. NAVY'S LARGEST ORDNANCE PRODUCER DURING WORLD WAR II.

MANY LEADING ADMIRALS CREDITED HAWLEY'S SUPERIOR PRODUCTS AND AHEAD-OF-SCHEDULE DELIVERIES WITH ENABLING THEM TO WIN THE "VICTORY AT SEA" AFTER THE GREAT JAPANESE HEAD START.

FOLLOWING THE WAR, MR. HAWLEY TURNED HIS INTERESTS TO OIL DRILLING AND HIT "GUSHERS" IN MONTANA AND TEXAS. WHEN ONE OF HIS COLORADO FARMLANDS INHABITED BY HEREFORD CATTLE CAME UP DRY, HE TRANSPORTED THEM TO McHENRY, ILLINOIS, WHERE HIS SON HELPS OVERSEE AN AWARD WINNING HERD.

NORTHERN ORDNANCE WAS SOLD TO FMC CORP. IN 1964. MR. HAWLEY DIED IN 1980 LEAVING NORTHERN PUMP TO BE OPERATED BY A TRUST FOR THE HAWLEY FAMILY.

GRANT'S
You Better Believe it!

COMING ORIGINALLY FROM NEW ULM, TIPPI HEDREN WAS RAISED IN MINNEAPOLIS WHERE SHE WENT TO WEST HIGH SCHOOL.

SHE BECAME A MODEL AND SALES PERSON FOR DONALDSON'S DEPARTMENT STORE.

WHEN HER FAMILY MOVED TO LOS ANGELES, TIPPI CONTINUED HER MODELING WHILE STUDYING ART AT PASADENA CITY COLLEGE

Tippi Hedren

LATER SHE TRAVERSED THE COUNTRY TO NEW YORK WHERE SHE LANDED A JOB IMMEDIATELY. FOR THE NEXT EIGHT YEARS SHE WAS ONE OF AMERICA'S TOP FASHION AND TELEVISION MODELS.

AFTER SEEING HER ON A COMMERCIAL DURING THE "TODAY" SHOW, DIRECTOR-PRODUCER ALFRED HITCHCOCK WAS IMPRESSED TO THE EXTENT THAT HE SIGNED HER TO A CONTRACT. HE STARRED HER IN TWO MOVIES, "MARNIE", AND "THE BIRDS."

SHE LATER BECAME DISENCHANTED WITH THE MOVIE INDUSTRY, INCLUDING HER PERSONAL RELATIONSHIP WITH HITCHCOCK, AND IS NOW INVOLVED IN ANIMAL RIGHTS CAUSES IN LOS ANGELES WHERE SHE STILL LIVES.

GRANT'S You Better Believe it!

WILLIAM WALTER "PUDGE" HEFFELFINGER WAS BORN IN MINNEAPOLIS.

WHILE ATTENDING CENTRAL HIGH SCHOOL HE ATTRACTED ATTENTION BY RUNNING THE "100" IN 11 SECONDS WEARING FOOTBALL GEAR. HE WENT ON TO COLLEGE AT YALE WHERE, AFTER A ROUGH FRESHMAN INITIATION, HE MADE THE TEAM. THIS BEGAN AN ERA DURING WHICH YALE OVERWHELMED THEIR OPPONENTS 698-0.

1889 WAS THE FIRST YEAR ALL-AMERICANS WERE PICKED AND PUDGE HEADED THE LIST. HE MADE ALL-AMERICAN THE NEXT TWO YEARS TOO, IN ADDITION TO HAVING BEEN PLACED ON EVERY ALL-TIME-ALL-AMERICAN TEAM PICKED SINCE.

HE WAS THE VERY FIRST EVER PRO-FOOTBALL PLAYER, RECEIVING $500 FOR ONE GAME.

WHEN 48 YEARS OLD HE PUT ON A UNIFORM TO GIVE THE YALE COACH SOME ASSISTANCE. AT THIS PRACTICE SESSION HE WOUND UP PUTTING FIVE OF YALE'S BEST LINE-MEN OUT OF COMMISSION. AT AGE 53 HE PLAYED ALL BUT FOUR MINUTES ON A TEAM OF "OLD STARS" WHICH BEAT THE OHIO STATE "GREATS" 16-0. AT 65 HE PLAYED HIS LAST FOOTBALL GAME WITH SEMI-PROS AGAINST ST. THOMAS ALUMNI. BEING ABLE ONLY TO PLAY PART OF THE GAME, HE DECIDED IT WOULD BE HIS LAST

Pudge Heffelfinger
1867-1954

AS HENNEPIN COUNTY COMMIS-IONER HE HELPED MAKE IT ONE OF THE FEW "DEBT FREE" COUNTIES IN THE NATION. HE ALSO ESTAB-LISHED HIS "PET PROJECT," THE MENDOTA BRIDGE.

AL PAPAS Jr.

GRANT'S
You Better Believe it!

THIS LEGENDARY EARLY-DAY ST. PAUL RAILROAD MAN WAS KNOWN THROUGHOUT THE UNITED STATES AS "THE EMPIRE BUILDER." HE WAS CREDITED WITH INTRODUCING MANY NEW INNOVATIONS TO RAILROADING, WITH HIS MASTER-KEY BEING "TRANSPORTATION SEEKS THE LINE OF LEAST RESISTANCE."

HIS GREAT NORTHERN RAILROAD BECAME THE "UNOFFICIAL SCHOOL OF AMERICAN RAILROADING," WITH THE MOST SUCCESSFULL MANAGERS IN THE UNITED STATES DRAWING THEIR FIRST INSPIRATION AND LEARNING FROM HILL.

JAMES J. HILL
1838-1916

HILL WAS CREDITED WITH BUILDING THE LARGEST AND MOST EFFECTIVE TERMINAL FACILITIES IN THE WORLD, AT THE HEAD OF LAKE SUPERIOR.

HE WAS ALSO ACTIVE IN BRINGING CATTLE TO THIS COUNTRY FROM ENGLAND, AND HIMSELF RAISED NATIONAL CHAMPION STOCK OF SEVERAL BREEDS AT HIS FARM IN NORTH OAKS. MOST HISTORIANS ARE IN AGREEMENT THAT THE AGRICULTURAL INTERESTS OF THE UNITED STATES OWE A LASTING DEBT TO THE ENTHUSIASM AND LIFE-LONG LABORS OF JAMES J. HILL.

GRANT'S You Better Believe it!

AL PAPAS Jr.

ST. PAUL'S HOLMAN FIELD WAS NAMED AFTER THIS MINNEAPOLIS FLYER EXTRA- ORDINAIRE.

ORIGINALLY A DAREDEVIL MOTORCYCLE RACER, SKILLFUL STUNT PILOT, AND WING- WALKER, HE EVOLVED INTO A NATIONALLY RENOWNED WINNER OF AIR RACES.

Charles W. "Speed" Holman

IN 1927 HE WON THE NEW YORK TO SPOKANE AIR DERBY, AND IN 1928 TOOK THE YEISER TROPHY FOR THE TIME FROM LOS ANGELES TO CINNCINATTI. IN 1929 HE WON THE GARDNER TROPHY RACE FROM ST. LOUIS TO INDIANAPOLIS AND BACK. IT WAS DESIGNED TO COINCIDE WITH THE INDIANAPOLIS MOTOR RACE.

HIS BIGGEST WIN OF ALL WAS THE UNLIMITED AIR RACING TITLE IN 1930. A YEAR LATER HE WAS KILLED DURING A PERFORMANCE AT A FAIR IN OMAHA, NEBRASKA. HIS FUNERAL WAS ONE OF THE LARGEST EVER HELD IN MINNESOTA AND WAS ATTENDED BY 100,000 PEOPLE.

HOLMAN WAS ALSO AN EARLY AIR MAIL PILOT FOR NORTHWEST AIR- LINES, AND SET MANY TIME RECORDS. HE WAS ALSO A CONFIDANTE OF CHARLES LINDBERGH, EDDIE RICKENBACKER, AND JIMMY DOOLITTLE.

GRANT'S You Better Believe it!

ONE OF THE NATION'S PREMIER PIONEERS IN BROADCASTING AND AVIATION...

STANLEY E. HUBBARD

HE WENT TO SCHOOL IN ST. PAUL AND LATER SERVED IN A FIELD SIGNAL BATTALION IN WWI. AFTER THE WAR HE ORGANIZED THE COUNTRIES' FIRST COMMERCIAL AIRLINE AND ESTABLISHED THE FIRST COMMUNICATION BETWEEN PLANES. IN 1923 HE LAID OUT THE AIR ROUTES BETWEEN CHICAGO AND NEW YORK WHICH COMMERCIAL AIRLINES STILL USE.

IN 1924 HUBBARD ESTABLISHED THE FIRST COMMERCIAL RADIO STATION IN THE NATION. BEING ABLE TO BROADCAST COAST TO COAST IN THE EARLY DAYS HE STARTED OUT SUCH STARS AS "SAM 'N' HENRY" (LATER TO BECOME "AMOS 'N' ANDY") JACK BENNY, EDGAR BERGEN, EDDIE ALBERT AND THE MARX BROTHERS.

KSTP, CHANNEL 5, WAS THE FIRST LOCAL TV STATION, GOING ON THE AIR APRIL 27, 1948, AND WAS THIRD IN THE ENTIRE COUNTRY. IT WAS FIRST WITH COLOR IN 1961 AND WITH A FULL-TIME NEWSROOM AND MOBILE TELECASTS.

HUBBARD ALSO HELPED RESCUE THE COMO ZOO, AND DEVELOP THE ST. PAUL WINTER CARNIVAL, THE MINNESOTA ZOOLOGICAL GARDENS, AND BOYS RANCH PROGRAM IN AUSTIN MINNESOTA.

THE INFANT DAYS OF HUBBARD'S LIVE SPORTS COVERAGE SAW A BABY CARRIAGE TRANSPORT A KSTP TRANSMITTER AT THE 1930 NATIONAL OPEN IN ST. PAUL.

GRANT'S You Better Believe it!

AL PAPAS Jr.

HUBERT H. HUMPHREY WAS BORN IN WALLACE, SOUTH DAKOTA.

HE STUDIED PHARMACY AT DENVER COLLEGE AND THEN WORKED IN HIS FATHERS DRUG STORE. IN 1939 HE CAME TO MINNESOTA AND RECEIVED SEVERAL HONORS WHILE DOING POST GRAD WORK AT THE U of M.

HE RAN FOR MAYOR OF MINNE-APOLIS IN 1943 AND WAS DE-FEATED, BUT CAME BACK AGAIN IN 1945 AND CAPTURED THE OFFICE.

HUMPHREY RAN FOR AND WON A SEAT IN THE U.S. SENATE IN 1948 AND SERVED THERE UNTIL 1964.

Hubert H. Humphrey 1911-1978

IN 1964 LYNDON JOHNSON SELECTED HIM TO BE HIS RUNNING MATE. AFTER SERVING AS VICE-PRESIDENT HE BECAME THE DEMOCRATIC NOMINEE FOR PRESIDENT IN 1968. IT WAS ONE OF THE CLOSEST ELECT-IONS IN HISTORY, BUT HE LOST TO RICHARD NIXON.

HE REGAINED HIS SENATE SEAT AND WAS ELECTED MAJORITY WHIP. HE HELD THAT POSITION UNTIL HE WAS STRICKEN BY CANCER AND DIED IN 1978. HE HAD CHOSEN TO BE LAID TO REST IN MINNEAPOLIS LAKEWOOD CEMETERY WHERE HIS EARLY IDOL AND INSPIRATION, GOVERNOR FLOYD B. OLSON, LIES BURIED NEARBY.

GRANT'S You Better Believe it!

ARCHBISHOP JOHN IRELAND WAS FOR MANY YEARS PRIOR TO THE "TURN OF THE CENTURY," ONE OF THE GREAT CHURCH LEADERS OF AMERICA. HIS EARLY PROMOTION OF IMMIGRATION TO MINNESOTA AND THE SETTLEMENT OF CATHOLIC COMMUNITIES THROUGHOUT THE ENTIRE STATE RESULTED IN HIS ARCHDIOCESE BECOMING ONE OF THE LARGEST IN THE COUNTRY. MUCH OF HIS SUCCESS WAS DUE TO J.J. HILL WHOSE COOPERATION RESULTED IN HIS BEING NAMED A "LAND AGENT" BY FIVE DIFFERENT RAILROADS.

AL PÃPAS Jr.

Archbishop John Ireland

ALTHOUGH HE FILLED MANY DIFFERENT ROLES AS A CHURCHMAN, SOCIAL REFORMER, EDUCATOR, AND PART-TIME INTERNATIONAL DIPLOMAT, HIS PRIMARY ROLE WAS AS BISHOP OF SAINT PAUL. AS SUCH HE MADE MINNESOTA THE CENTER OF THE CATHOLIC CULTURE FOR THE ENTIRE MIDWEST.

HIS AGGRESSIVE NATURE AND INVOLVEMENT IN NATIONAL POLITICS PLAYED AN IMPORTANT PART IN SEVERAL ELECTIONS. WHILE HIS ORIGINAL GOAL WAS TO RECRUIT FARMERS, MANY OF THE PERSONS OF IRISH DESCENT WHO ANSWERED HIS CALL HAD SAVINGS AND BECAME SUCCESSFULL BUSINESS MEN IN OTHER FIELDS OF ENDEAVOR. SOME OF THOSE FAMILIES ARE STILL PROMINENT IN SAINT PAUL TODAY.

GRANT'S
You Better Believe it!

BORN IN MINNEAPOLIS, IRWIN JACOBS GREW UP ON THE NORTH SIDE WHERE HE GRADUATED FROM NORTH HIGH SCHOOL.

HE WENT TO WORK FOR N.W. BAG, A FAMILY-OWNED BUSINESS.

EARLY ON HE BECAME INTERESTED IN JOB LOT CLOSE-OUTS, AND SUCCESSFULLY MERCHANDISED A VARIETY OF THOSE SALES GOODS.

HE FIRST SURFACED AS A PROMINENT BUSINESS MAN IN CONJUNCTION WITH HIS ACQUISITION OF MINNEAPOLIS GRAIN BELT BREWERIES. TODAY HE IS WELL KNOWN THROUGHOUT THE FINANCIAL WORLD AS A "CORPORATE RAIDER", HAVING BECOME INVOLVED IN SCORES OF NATIONALLY-KNOWN "CORPORATIONS BY BUYING UP MINORITY STOCK HOLDINGS. JACOBS IS CONSIDERED EITHER A "FINANCIAL GENIUS" OR A "PIRATE" DEPENDING ON WHO YOU ARE TALKING TO.

HIS PROXY FIGHTS HAVE HAD GOVERNORS AND SENATORS LINED UP ON OPPOSITE SIDES OF THE FENCE. THE MERE RUMOR THAT HE IS INTERESTED IN A CERTAIN CORPORATION HAS BEEN KNOWN TO CAUSE GREAT STOCK MOVEMENT.

Irwin L. Jacobs

GARRISON KEILLOR

...IS A ST. PAUL NATIVE WHO GOT HIS START AS A HUMORIST ON MINNESOTA PUBLIC RADIO BEFORE WRITING HIS BEST SELLING "LAKE WOBEGON DAYS."

SOME OF HIS DYED-IN-THE-WOOL FANS WOULD SEEMINGLY WALK THROUGH "BROKEN GLASS" TO SEE HIM OR OBTAIN AN AUTOGRAPH. OTHERS VIEW HIM AS INCONSIDERATE LOUT WHO THINKS NOTHING OF BEING LATE OR FAILING TO SHOW FOR APPEARANCES.

HIS BRAND OF HUMOR MIGHT BE DESCRIBED AS "MODERN DAY WILL ROGERS" WITH A LITTLE MORE BITE TO IT.

AL PĀPAS Jr.

GRANT'S You Better Believe it!

NOT ALWAYS DIVERSIFIED IN HIS HUMOROUS APPROACH, HE HAS SEEMED TO MAINTAIN AN OBSESSION WITH "POWDER-MILK BISCUITS," AND BASEBALL.

HIS PLAY ON NAMES AND NOSTALGIA EVENTS BELIES THE GENIUS THAT HAS SKI-ROCKETED KEILLOR INTO A NATIONAL FIGURE WITH HIS "PRAIRIE HOME RADIO" EMINATING FROM DOWNTOWN ST. PAUL. WHILE STILL NOT A MULTI-MILLIONAIRE, HIS IDENTITY IS NOW SUCH THAT ANY OF HIS OFFERINGS ARE READILY ACKNOWLEDGED BY HIS FANS ALL OVER THE UNITED STATES.

GRANT'S **You Better Believe it!**

RED HAIRED STAR OF THE "LOU GRANT" TV SHOW...

Linda Kelsey

...WAS EMMY-NOMINATED FOR HER PART IN IT AS THE REPORTER, BILLIE NEWMAN.

LINDA ATTENDED ST. PAUL'S WASHINGTON HIGH SCHOOL WHERE SHE FIRST BECAME INVOLVED IN DRAMATICS. LATER SHE ATTENDED THE "U OF M" PARTICIPATING IN THE "SHOWBOAT." CHANHASSEN DINNER THEATRE, THE GUTHRIE, AND THE CHILDREN'S THEATRE WERE ADDITIONAL STEPPING STONES TO PARTS ON "THE ROOKIES," "ROCKFORD FILES" AND M·A·S·H TV SHOWS.

LINDA IS MARRIED TO CBS PUBLICIST GLEN STRAND, AND HER FATHER IS STILL A PRACTICING DENTIST IN ST. PAUL.

AL PAPAS Jr.

GRANT'S You Better Believe it!

FAMED POLIO FIGHTER, SISTER ELIZABETH KENNY, CAME TO MINNEAPOLIS IN 1940. HERE SHE FOUND A COOPERATIVE COMMUNITY, UNLIKE THE COOL RECEPTION SHE HAD RECEIVED ON HER ARRIVAL IN CALIFORNIA.

BY 1942 A SISTER KENNY INSTITUTE WAS FOUNDED AT 1800 CHICAGO AVENUE, AND SHE WAS BUSILY ENGAGED IN IMPARTING HER TECHNIQUES TO OTHERS. IN 1943 A FOUNDATION WAS FORMED TO SUPPORT HER WORK.

AL PAPAS JR.

Sister Elizabeth Kenny

1886–1952

THE TWIN CITIES AREA SUFFERED A SEVERE POLIO OUTBREAK IN 1946. WITH THE THEN MAYOR HUBERT HUMPHREY LEADING THE WAY, THE INSTITUTE AIDED MANY VICTIMS. IN THAT SAME YEAR THE MOVIE "SISTER KENNY," STARRING ROSALIND RUSSELL (WHOSE OWN SON HAD BEEN AFFLICTED) WAS RELEASED. SISTER KENNY'S FAME WAS THEN PERMANENTLY SECURE.

WITH HER WORK IN THE UNITED STATES WELL IN HAND, SHE RETURNED TO HER HOME IN AUSTRALIA IN 1950. SHE DIED TWO YEARS AFTER THEN. IRONICALLY, SHE HERSELF WAS PARTIALLY PARALYZED IN HER LATER YEARS.

TODAY THERE IS A NEW SISTER KENNY INSTITUTE BUILDING WITH A SKYWAY CONNECTING IT TO ABBOTT-NORTHWESTERN HOSPITAL.

GRANT'S *You Better Believe it!*

THE FIRST MINNESOTA
TWIN TO MAKE IT TO THE
BASEBALL HALL OF FAME
STARTED HIS MAJOR LEAGUE
CAREER IN 1954. HE WAS
THE FIRST EVER BONUS
PLAYER IN THE GRIFFITH
ORGANIZATION.

OUTSIDE OF BASEBALL HE
PLAYED QUARTERBACK IN
HIGH SCHOOL FOOTBALL AND
GOT MANY COLLEGE OFFERS
TO PLAY.

HARMON KILLEBREW

MOSTLY KNOWN FOR HIS HOME RUNS THE "KILLER" LED THE AMERICAN
LEAGUE SIX TIMES. TWICE HE HIT 49 HOMERS IN A SEASON. IN 1962 HE
TIED A MAJOR LEAGUE MARK BY HITTING TWO OR MORE ROUND TRIPPERS
IN EACH LEAGUE PARK. IN THAT SAME YEAR HE GOT TOGETHER WITH
BOB ALLISON TO EACH HIT GRAND SLAMS IN THE SAME INNING AGAINST
CLEVELAND. THIS WAS A MAJOR LEAGUE FIRST. HE SET THE AMERICAN
LEAGUE RECORD FOR THE MOST HOMERS (573 LIFETIME) BY A RIGHT
HANDED BATTER AND THE MOST BASES ON BALLS (160 LIFETIME).
KILLEBREW'S HOME RUN RATIO OF ONE EVERY 12.99 TIMES AT BAT REMAINS
SECOND ONLY TO BABE RUTH WHO HIT ONE EVERY 11.76 TIMES AT BAT.
HARMON ALSO ESTABLISHED A MAJOR LEAGUE RECORD FOR THE MOST
YEARS (3) WITH NO STOLEN BASES IN 150 OR MORE GAMES. HE WAS
NAMED TO 11 ALL-STAR TEAMS AND WAS THE AMERICAN LEAGUE MOST
VALUABLE PLAYER IN 1969.

GRANT'S You Better Believe it!

JOAN MANSFIELD KROC GREW UP ON ST. PAUL'S WEST SIDE AND GRADUATED FROM HUMBOLDT HIGH SCHOOL. SHE WAS AN OUTSTANDING SPEED SKATER PARTICIPATING FOR THE LAKE COMO TEAM IN CONJUNCTION WITH THE ST. PAUL WINTER CARNIVAL.

SHE BECAME AN EXCELLENT ORGANIST PERFORMING FOR KSTP, AND LATER THE CRITER- ION ON UNIVERSITY AVENUE. THERE SHE MET RAY KROC, HER FUTURE HUSBAND, AND OWNER OF THE VAST INTERNATIONAL McDONALD'S FAST FOOD CHAIN.

Joan Kroc

WHEN MR. KROC PASSED AWAY RECENTLY, SHE SUCCEEDED HIM AS HEAD OF McDONALDS AND THE SAN DIEGO PADRES BASEBALL TEAM, WHICH HE HAD ALSO OWNED.

TODAY SHE IS ALSO A NATIONAL LEADER IN THE TREATMENT OF CHEMICAL DEPENDENCY HEADING UP "OPERATION CORK" (WHICH IS KROC SPELLED BACKWARDS). JOAN IS ALSO A LARGE CONTRIBUTOR TO HAZELDEN FOUND- ATION WHOSE SUPERBLY-EQUIPPED FACILITY IN CENTER CITY, MINNESOTA, SPECIALIZES IN TREATMENT OF PERSONS CONNECTED WITH SPORTS.

SHE IS ALSO INVOLVED IN MOTION PICTURE PRODUCTIONS, A RECENT ONE BEING "MASS APPEAL" STARRING JACK LEMMON.

JOHN H. MAC MILLAN, JR. WAS FORMER BOARD CHAIRMAN OF CARGILL, INC. FROM 1932-1960. HE WAS CARGILL'S CHIEF ORGANIZER AS WELL AS CHIEF INVENTOR. HIS INCREDIBLE INGENUITY BROUGHT FORTH TOTALLY NEW DESIGNS FOR GRAIN ELEVATORS, BARGE EQUIPMENT, AND OCEAN-GOING VESSELS. HIS UNCANNY "FORESIGHT" IN EVERY DIRECTION RESULTED IN TWIN CITIES LOCAL CARGILL COMPANY BECOMING A WORLD LEADER IN ALL AREAS IN WHICH IT COMPETES.

John H. MacMillan, Jr.

SINCE HIS PASSING IN 1960, A SUCCESSION OF OUTSTANDING CARGILLS AND MAC MILLANS HAVE EMERGED TO PICK UP WHERE HE LEFT OFF. IT IS CONCEDED BY MOST THAT HIS ALMOST DIVINE TALENTS WERE THE CATALYST THAT TODAY MAKES CARGILL THE WORLDS LEADER IN GRAIN EXPORTS; SECOND IN BEEF PACKING; THIRD IN EGG PRODUCING, CORN MILLING, AND WHEAT MILLING. IT IS ALSO A MAJOR LEADER IN SOYBEAN CRUSHING, COFFEE TRADING, AND EVEN STEEL MILLS.

GRANT'S
You Better Believe it!

... HE CAME TO PLAY HOCKEY AND
FOOTBALL. AS A DEFENSEMAN IN
HOCKEY HE ATTAINED ALL-AMERICAN
HONORS IN 1940.

JOHN THEN ENTERED PRO HOCKEY
WITH THE CHICAGO BLACKHAWKS. HE
LEFT THEM DURING WORLD WAR II TO
SERVE IN THE COAST GUARD AND
RETURNED AFTERWARD TO COMPLETE
HIS PLAYING CAREER.

JOHN MARIUCCI

NEXT HE JOINED THE MINNESOTA GOPHERS AS COACH FOR 14 SEASONS. HE
WAS STRONG ON DEVELOPING AMERICAN TALENT ON HIS TEAMS RATHER
THAN IMPORTING CANADIANS. HE WAS ALSO A U.S. OLYMPIC TEAM COACH.

HEADING BACK TO THE PROS HE JOINED THE MINNESOTA NORTH STARS AS
A SCOUT. OTHER DUTIES FOR THE STARS HAVE FOUND HIM ACTING AS TRAVEL-
ING SECRETARY AND COACH DURING EMERGENCIES. HE IS NOW ASSISTANT
GENERAL MANAGER.

THE FORMER WILLIAMS ARENA RINK ON THE MINNESOTA CAMPUS HAS
RECENTLY BEEN RENAMED "MARIUCCI ARENA." OTHER HONORS, FOR JOHN,
ARE HIS INDUCTION INTO THE "UNITED STATES HOCKEY HALL OF FAME,"
AND THE NATIONAL "HOCKEY HALL OF FAME."

AL PAPAS Jr.

GRANT'S You Better Believe it!

THIS TWIN CITIES NATIVE ENTERED THE HOLLYWOOD CIRCUIT AS A MOVIE PRODUCER VIA HIS "PERSONALS," "HOT DOG," AND MOST RECENTLY "YOUNGBLOOD." HIS SECOND "HOT DOG" EARNED $21,000,000 ENABLING HIM TO MAKE "YOUNGBLOOD." HIS FIRST FILM, "PERSONALS," WAS MADE ENTIRELY IN MINNEAPOLIS, INCLUDING MANY LAKE SCENES THAT ARE RECOGNIZABLE TO LOCAL RESIDENTS. HE PRESENTLY IS EVALUATING OTHER SCRIPTS AND PLANS SEVERAL FUTURE PRODUCTIONS.

PETER MARKLE

MARKLE, AN ABOVE-AVERAGE HOCKEY PLAYER HIMSELF AT BLAKE AND LATER IN COLLEGE AT YALE, IS CREDITED WITH BRINGING THE GAME TO THE SCREEN AS IT REALLY IS IN "YOUNGBLOOD." HE REPAID HIS OLD ALMA MATER, BLAKE, BY STAGING A PREMIERE BENEFIT WHICH PROVIDED FUNDS TO RENOVATE THE RINK THERE.

GRANT'S You Better Believe it!

McCARTHY RECEIVED HIS MASTER OF ARTS DEGREE FROM THE UofM IN 1938. HE WAS ACTING HEAD OF THE SOCIOLOGY DEPARTMENT AT SAINT THOMAS COLLEGE WHEN ELECTED TO THE U.S. CONGRESS IN 1948.

Eugene McCarthy

HE WAS RE-ELECTED TO CONGRESS FOUR TIMES WHEN IN 1958 HE WAS ELECTED TO THE U.S. SENATE. WHILE IN THE SENATE HE SERVED ON MANY COMMITTEES, INCLUDING HEAD OF THE FOREIGN RELATIONS COMMITTEE IN 1965.

IN 1968 McCARTHY RAN FOR PRESIDENT. HIS SUPPORTERS WERE CREDITED WITH DISRUPTING THE DEMOCRATIC CONVENTION THAT YEAR TO THE EXTENT IT COST HIS FORMER FRIEND AND ALLY, HUBERT HUMPHREY, HIS OWN BID FOR THE PRESIDENCY.

HAVING RETIRED FROM THE SENATE IN 1970 McCARTHY SETTLED IN THE BLUE RIDGE MOUNTAINS OF VIRGINIA WHERE HE HAS WRITTEN SEVERAL BOOKS PUBLISHED BY DOUBLEDAY.

GRANT'S You Better Believe it!

WILLIAM L. McKNIGHT WAS ORIGINALLY FROM SOUTH DAKOTA. AFTER WORKING HARVESTING JOBS, AND GRADUATING FROM HIGH SCHOOL, HE MOVED TO DULUTH, MINNESOTA. THERE HE STAYED WITH RELATIVES AND ATTENDED A BUSINESS UNIVERSITY.

OFFERED A JOB BY 3M, THEN A "STRUGGLING" SANDPAPER MANUFACTURER, HE SOON LEARNED OF THEIR SHAKY POSITION. HE CONCERNED HIMSELF WITH HOW TO MAKE BETTER SANDPAPER AND CUT COSTS AT THE SAME TIME.

AL PAPAS JR.

William L. McKnight
1887 - 1978

TWO YEARS LATER HE WAS SENT TO THEIR CHICAGO OFFICE AS MANAGER AND ASSISTANT TO THE SALES MANAGER.

AFTER PERSONALLY GETTING INVOLVED IN BOTH "QUALITY CONTROL," AND SALES, BUSINESS SOARED AND McKNIGHT WAS MADE VICE-PRESIDENT. FROM THAT POINT HE SAW HIS $500 LABORATORY DEVELOPED INTO A 180 MILLION DOLLAR A YEAR RESEARCH OPERATION COVERING MANY TECHNOLOGIES WITH HIM AT THE TOP OF 3M.

TODAY 3M IS ONE OF THE LARGEST COMPANIES IN THE WORLD, AND HOLD INNUMERABLE PATENTS ON MANY DIVERSE PRODUCTS.

GRANT'S You Better Believe it!

"MR. BASKETBALL" WAS BORN IN JOLIET, ILLINOIS.

AS A BOY HE GOT A COMPOUND FRACTURE TO HIS LEG AND WAS TOLD HE WOULD NEVER PLAY BASKETBALL AGAIN. THOUGH HE DIDN'T PLAY BALL IN HIGH SCHOOL HE RECEIVED HONORABLE MENTION ALL-AMERICAN AT DE PAUL UNIVERSITY IN HIS FRESHMAN YEAR AND OUTRIGHT ALL-AMERICAN THE FOLLOWING THREE YEARS. HE AVERAGED 19.8 POINTS PER GAME

GEORGE MIKAN

MIKAN CAME TO MINNEAPOLIS IN 1947 TO JOIN THE LAKERS. THE FOLLOWING YEAR HE WAS NAMED THEIR MOST VALUABLE PLAYER WHILE LEADING THEM TO THEIR FIRST CHAMPIONSHIP. THERE CAME SIX CHAMPIONSHIPS OUT OF SEVEN YEARS. BY 1952 HE WAS NAMED THE "GREATEST BASKETBALL PLAYER OF THE FIRST HALF-CENTURY." AS A PRO HE SCORED 11,764 POINTS FOR AN AVERAGE OF 22.6 PER GAME.

AFTER RETIRING FROM PLAYING BASKETBALL HE ENTERED LAW PRACTICE AND THE TRAVEL BUSINESS IN WHICH HE IS STILL INVOLVED. AT THE PRESENT TIME HE IS ALSO A PART OF A GROUP WHO ARE ATTEMPTING TO RETURN PRO BASKETBALL TO THE TWIN CITIES.

GRANT'S You Better Believe it!

THE MILWAUKEE BREWERS SUPER STAR BASEBALL PLAYER WAS BORN IN ST. PAUL.

HE WENT TO CRETIN HIGH SCHOOL AND LATER TO THE U oF M. IN COLLEGE HE CONSISTENTLY HIT JUST UNDER .400 AND WAS AN OUTSTANDING "BASE STEALER." HE WAS NAMED TO THE ALL-AMERICAN TEAM.

Paul Molitor

MOLITOR WAS DRAFTED BY THE BREWERS IN 1977, AND WAS THE FIRST PLAYER IN HISTORY TO PLAY AT FOUR DIFFERENT POSITIONS: CENTERFIELD, SECOND BASE, THIRD BASE, AND SHORTSTOP, BECOMING THE MOST VERSATILE PLAYER IN A DECADE.

HIS NEWEST CONTRACT WITH MILWAUKEE HAS PLACED HIM IN THE MULTI-MILLIONAIRE CLASS.

GRANT'S You Better Believe it!

BORN IN CEYLON MINNE-
SOTA, WALTER F. MONDALE
ATTENDED THE U of M LAW
SCHOOL GRADUATING IN
1951 WITH HONORS.

HE ENTERED PRIVATE
PRACTICE IN THE TWIN
CITIES FROM 1956-1960.
FROM 1960-1964 HE WAS
MINNESOTA'S ATTORNEY
GENERAL.

AL PAPAS Jr.

WALTER F. MONDALE

NEXT HE SERVED AS UNITED STATES SENATOR FOR 13 YEARS. HE
BECAME VICE-PRESIDENT OF THE UNITED STATES UNDER JAMES
CARTER FROM 1977-1980. BEING NOMINATED FOR PRESIDENT IN
1984, BY THE DEMOCRATIC PARTY, HE LOST TO RONALD REAGAN
IN THE GENERAL ELECTION. MONDALE IS NOW IN PRIVATE LAW
PRACTICE.

GRANT'S *You Better Believe it!*

THE ALL-STAR PITCHER FOR THE DETROIT TIGERS BASEBALL TEAM, JACK MORRIS, GRADUATED FROM ST. PAUL'S HIGHLAND PARK HIGH SCHOOL IN 1973.

HE LATER ATTENDED BRIGHAM YOUNG UNIVERSITY FROM WHENCE HE WAS SIGNED BY THE TIGERS.

Jack Morris

BREAKING INTO THE TIGER ROTATION IN 1977 HE HAS BEEN A SUPER STAR EVER SINCE, EARNING JUST UNDER A MILLION DOLLARS PER YEAR.

HIS ORIGINAL CONTRACT HAS EXPIRED. AS A FREE AGENT IT HAS BEEN PREDICTED HE WILL NOW COMMAND A SALARY OF ONE AND ONE-HALF MILLION YEARLY.

Grant's You Better Believe it!

COMING TO THE TWIN CITIES FROM INTERNATIONAL FALLS, BRONISLAU "BRONKO" NAGURSKI LEFT AGAIN AFTER BECOMING THE LIVING LEGEND OF FOOTBALL. ON OFFENSE HE WAS AN ALL-AMERICAN FULL-BACK AND ON DEFENSE AN ALL-AMERICAN TACKLE. HE WAS THE ONLY PLAYER EVER TO RECEIVE SUCH DUAL RECOGNITION. KNOWN FOR HIS HARD HITTING, OTHER TEAMS WERE FORCED TO GANG TACKLE HIM.

BRONKO NAGURSKI

AFTER LEAVING THE U OF M HE PLAYED WITH RED GRANGE FOR THE CHICAGO BEARS. ACCURATE STATISTICS WERE NOT KEPT THEN, BUT HE IS CREDITED WITH 4,031 YARDS IN 872 CARRIES FOR A 4.6 YARD AVERAGE. THIS WAS ALMOST ALL THROUGH A STACKED LINE. HE WAS KNOWN TO PASS FOR A COUPLE TOUCHDOWNS IN THE CHAMPIONSHIP GAME AGAINST THE GIANTS IN 1933. IN 1937 HE RETIRED TO BECOME A PRO WRESTLER. THE BEARS CALLED HIM BACK TO PLAY ONE EXTRA SEASON IN 1943 WHEN HE WAS 35.

BRONKO WAS UNANIMOUSLY ELECTED TO THE NATIONAL FOOTBALL HALL OF FAME, ALL-TIME ALL-BIG TEN, AND MODERN ALL-TIME TEAM 1920-1969. OTHER SPORTS HE EXCELLED IN WERE THE DISCUS, SHOT-PUT AND BASKETBALL.

HE PLAYED HIS LAST FOOTBALL IN THE GOPHER ALUMNI GAME OF 1960. THOUGH IN HIS 50'S HE PLUNGED AND CARRIED PLAYERS ON HIS BACK WHO WOULD BE THE BACKBONE OF A NATIONAL CHAMPIONSHIP TEAM... HE STILL GOT HIS YARDAGE.

HIS WORK IS ON EXHI-
BITION IN FAMOUS
MUSEUMS AND GALLERIES
ALL OVER THE WORLD.

AL PAPAS JR.

LeRoy Neiman

GRANT'S
You
Better
Believe
it!

HE WAS BORN IN AND GREW UP IN ST. PAUL WHERE
HE WENT TO WASHINGTON HIGH SCHOOL. AFTER WWII,
WHERE HE EARNED FIVE BATTLE STARS, HE ATTENDED THE
ST. PAUL ART CENTER. NOW HE'S ONE OF THE WORLD'S LEADING COMMERCIAL ARTISTS.

THE "NEIMAN TECHNIQUE" CAPTURES THE "MOMENT OF HAPPENING" WHETHER
IT BE SPORTING EVENTS, THEATRE OPENINGS, POLITICAL EVENTS, THE GAMING
TABLES OF MONTE CARLO, OR THE BALLET. HE IS NOTED FOR HIS MAXIMUM
USE OF EVERY COLOR IN THE UNIVERSE.

GRANT'S
You Better Believe it!

CHAIRMAN EMERITUS AND FOUNDER OF CONTROL DATA CORPORATION:

WILLIAM C. NORRIS

ORIGINALLY NORRIS FOUNDED ENGINEER RESEARCH ASSOCIATES OF ST. PAUL AND LATER MERGED INTO SPERRY RAND UNIVAC WHICH HE HEADED UNTIL 1957. HE THEN LEFT TO START CONTROL DATA, NOW THE LEADING COMPANY IN LARGE-SCALE SCIENTIFIC ENGINEERING COMPUTERS AND COMPUTER SERVICES. IT HAS AN ANNUAL SALES OF FIVE-BILLION AND ASSETS OF SEVEN-BILLION DOLLARS.

MR. NORRIS IS A MEMBER OF MANY NATIONAL AND INTERNATIONAL ORGANIZATIONS AND IS A TRUSTEE OF THE UNIVERSITIES SPACE RESEARCH ASSOCIATION. HE IS IN DEMAND AS A SPEAKER BOTH IN THE UNITED STATES AND ABROAD.

HE ALSO FINDS TIME FOR HIS SIX SONS AND TWO DAUGHTERS PLUS 15 GRANDCHILDREN IN ADDITION TO HIS HOBBIES OF READING, FISHING, SWIMMING, AND WALKING IN THE MINNESOTA COUNTRYSIDE.

GRANT'S
You Better Believe it!

I. A. O'SHAUGHNESSY WAS A LEADING PHILANTHROPIST FROM ST. PAUL WHO GAVE $500,000 TO ST. CATHERINE'S COLLEGE AND BUILT O'SHAUGHNESSY AUDITORIUM, ONE OF THE STATE'S FINEST. IN 1942 HE GAVE $100,000 TO THE LIBERAL ARTS PROGRAM, AND ANOTHER $2,000,000 IN 1953 FOR A MEMORIAL LIBRARY THERE.

I.A. O'SHAUGHNESSY

HE CONTRIBUTED OVER $4,000,000 TOWARD AN EUCUNEMICAL INSTITUTE FOR ADVANCED THEOLOGICAL STUDY IN JERUSALEM WHICH OPENED IN 1964. POPE PAUL STATED "IT IS THE GREATEST THING THAT HAS HAPPENED IN MY REIGN."

O'SHAUGHNESSY WAS DECLARED MINNESOTA'S FOURTH RICHEST CITIZEN. HE PURCHASED ROSSE CASTLE IN COUNTY KERRY, IRELAND WHICH INCLUDED 3,000 ACRES OF LAND, 5,000 ACRES OF WATER IN ADDITION TO MOUNTAINS AND GOLF COURSES.

BESIDES HIS GENEROSITY HE ALSO POSSESSED A REAL AND CONSTANT WIT.

GRANT'S
You Better Believe it!

Gordon Parks

THE DIRECTOR OF THE BOX OFFICE
HIT "SHAFT" AND "SHAFT'S BIG
SCORE" WAS ORIGINALLY FROM KANSAS.
HE MOVED TO ST. PAUL AS A YOUTH
WHERE HE ATTENDED MECHANIC ARTS AND
CENTRAL. THESE TIMES WERE ROUGH
AS HE SOMETIMES LIVED ALONE WITH
NO PLACE TO SLEEP.

PARKS TRIED HIS HAND AT SEMI-PRO
BASKETBALL, SCULPTING AND PROSE WRITING.
HE DISCOVERED HIS LIFE WORK WHEN HE WAS
PROMPTED TO BUY HIS FIRST CAMERA FOR $12.50.
IN TWO MONTHS HE HAD HIS FIRST EXHIBIT IN MINNEAPOLIS.

HE WAS SUCCESSFUL DOING PORTRAITS OF SOCIETY WOMEN OF BOTH BLACK
AND WHITE RACES. HIS LEISURE TIME WAS SPENT WORKING ON PHOTOGRAPHIC
SCENES OF CHICAGO SOUTH SIDE POVERTY. THIS WAS A PROJECT CLOSE TO
HIS HEART WHICH GAVE HIM RECOGNITION. LIFE MAGAZINE EMPLOYED
HIM FROM 1948-1972.

BOOKS BY PARKS INCLUDE "THE LEARNING TREE," WHICH WAS MADE INTO
A MOVIE, AND "FLASH PHOTOGRAPHY," "CAMERA PORTRAITS," "A CHOICE
OF WEAPONS," "PHOTOS AND POEMS," AND "MOMENTS WITHOUT PROPER
NAMES."

JEANETTE PICCARD

1895-1981

ORIGINALLY FROM CHICAGO, SHE MOVED TO MINNEAPOLIS IN 1937.

JEANETTE PICCARD BECAME THE NATION'S PREMIER FEMALE BALLOONIST, SETTING AN ALTITUDE RECORD OF 57,559 FEET. N.A.S.A. STILL REFERS TO HER AS "THE FIRST WOMAN IN SPACE."

HER HUSBAND, JEAN, WAS DECENDED FROM A SWISS FAMILY WHO WERE LONG-INVOLVED IN BALLOON WORK. HE WAS THE FIRST TO USE MULTIPLE BALLOONS IN FLIGHT. THEIR SON, DON, ALSO HOLDS NUMEROUS RECORDS. THE ENTIRE FAMILY IS FEATURED IN THE ENCYCLOPEDIA BRITTANICA.

MADAME PICCARD, AFTER BEING NAMED AS A CONSULTANT TO N.A.S.A. MANNED SPACECRAFT CENTER, UTILIZED HER DIVERSITY BY BECOMING AN ORDAINED EPISCOPAL PRIEST.

AL PAPAS Jr.

GRANT'S You Better Believe it!

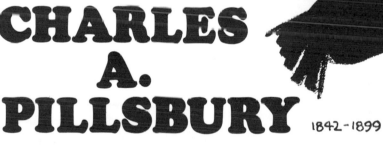

CHARLES A. PILLSBURY WAS FOUNDER OF THE PILLSBURY COMPANY.

HE CAME TO MINNEAPOLIS FROM NEW HAMPSHIRE IN 1869 AFTER GRADUATING FROM DARTMOUTH UNIVERSITY.

CHARLES A. PILLSBURY

1842-1899

AFTER LEARNING THE MILLING BUSINESS IN A PARTNERSHIP, HE MANAGED TO ACQUIRE MINNEAPOLIS FLOURING, AND ALASKA MILLS. THE NAME ALASKA MILLS WAS CHANGED TO PILLSBURY MILLS. HE THEN INTRODUCED NEW TECHNIQUES WHICH GAVE HIM A THREE DOLLAR BARREL EDGE OVER THE PREVIOUS MILLING LEADERS IN ST. LOUIS. PILLSBURY BECAME ONE OF THE COMMUNITY'S MOST POPULAR BUSINESS MEN.

SINCE HIS DEATH IN 1899 THE CONTINUED GROWTH OF HIS COMPANY HAS BEEN ASTRONOMICAL BUT NOT WITHOUT SOME TRYING TIMES. SOME OF THE PILLSBURY SUBSIDIARIES TODAY INCLUDE BURGER-KING, STEAK AND ALE, GREEN GIANT, HAAGEN DAZS ICE CREAM, AND TOTINOS PIZZA. THEIR MASCOT "THE PILLSBURY DOUGHBOY" IS RENOWNED FROM COAST-TO-COAST.

GRANT'S
You Better Believe it!

MARY ELLEN PINKHAM IS A MINNEAPOLIS BORN WEST HIGH GRADUATE.

HER BOOK "MARY ELLEN'S HELPFUL HINTS" SOLD TWELVE MILLION COPIES AND BECAME A NEW YORK TIMES BEST SELLER IN 1979-1980.

SINCE HER INITIAL PUBLICATION SHE HAS WRITTEN THREE ADDITIONAL BOOKS COVERING DIET, HEALTH, AND "HOW TO STOP THE ONE YOU LOVE FROM DRINKING." ALL HAVE HIT THE BEST SELLER LIST, INCLUDING TWO OF THEM AT ONE TIME.

MARY ELLEN PINKHAM

HER DIET BOOK COMMANDED THE HIGHEST ADVANCE OF ANY "HOW TO" EVER AT $775,000 BY SAINT MARTIN'S PRESS OF NEW YORK.

MARY ELLEN HAS BEEN A REGULAR ON THE ABC NETWORK "GOOD MORNING AMERICA" PROGRAM, APPEARING THREE TIMES WEEKLY.

SHE IS A NEW YORK TIMES SYNDICATED COLUMNIST APPEARING IN 200 NEWSPAPERS, IN ADDITION TO WRITING COLUMNS FOR "FAMILY CIRCLE" MAGAZINE AND "COSMOPOLITAN." TIME MAGAZINE HAS REFERRED TO HER AS "THE MOST PHENOMENALLY SUCCESSFUL WRITER OF THE PAST FIVE YEAR PERIOD.

GRANT'S You Better Believe it!

CARL POHLAD CAME TO MINNE-
APOLIS FROM IOWA.

HE WORKED HIS WAY UP IN
THE BANKING INDUSTRY AFTER
ENGAGING IN VARIOUS LABOR-
IOUS JOBS. AFTER SERVING AS
HEAD OF THE CHICAGO-LAKE
BANK, HE MOVED UP TO MARQUETTE
AND IS NOW PRESIDENT OF
MARQUETTE BANK, MINNEAPOLIS, N.A.

IN ADDITION TO BEING OWNER
OF THE MINNESOTA TWINS BASE-
BALL TEAM OF THE AMERICAN
LEAGUE, HE IS BOARD CHAIRMAN
OF M.E.I. DIVERSIFIED, INC., WHICH
ENCOMPASSES MANY NATIONALLY
KNOWN COMPANIES THROUGHOUT
THE UNITED STATES.

CARL POHLAD

THEY INCLUDE: PRICE CANDY, KANSAS CITY, MO., HADLEY DATE GARDENS,
THERMAL, CALIF., TEXAS AIR, T.G.I. FRIDAY'S, AZAR NUT, EL PASO, TEXAS,
BONNER PACKING, FRESNO, CALIF., PARKER PRODUCTS, INC., HOLLISTON,
MASS., ALL-AMERICAN NUT, CERRITOS, CALIF., AND FAIRHOPE NUT
PROCESSING, FAIRHOPE, ALABAMA.

POHLAD IS ALSO WELL KNOWN IN BOTTLING CIRCLES. ONLY RECENTLY
HE SOLD HIS PEPSI-COLA INTERESTS AFTER HAVING BEEN WRITTEN
UP IN WALL STREET JOURNAL AND OTHER PUBLICATIONS AS "BOTTLER
OF THE YEAR."

GRANT'S
You Better Believe it!

PRESIDING BISHOP OF THE
AMERICAN LUTHERAN CHURCH:

Dr. David W. Preus

DR. PREUS SERVED IN THE ARMY
SIGNAL INTELLIGENCE AFTER
GRADUATION FROM LUTHER
COLLEGE IN IOWA. AFTER THE
ARMY HE CAME TO MINNESOTA AND
WENT TO THE U OF M LAW SCHOOL
AND ENROLLED AT LUTHER SEM-
INARY IN ST. PAUL. HE GRADUATED
AND WAS ORDAINED IN 1950.
HIS EDUCATION PROCESS THEN TOOK HIM TO SCHOOLS THROUGHOUT THE
U.S. AND ENGLAND. HE CAME HOME AGAIN TO BE CAMPUS PASTOR AT THE
U OF M AND THE UNIVERSITY LUTHERAN CHURCH OF HOPE.

AS AN ADVOCATE FOR CHURCH MEMBERS TO PARTICIPATE IN CIVIC AND COM-
MUNITY AFFAIRS DR. PREUS HAS SERVED ON THE MINNEAPOLIS SCHOOL BOARD
WITH TWO OF HIS YEARS THERE AS ITS PRESIDENT. HE HAS SERVED ON MANY
OTHER COMMUNITY ORGANIZATIONS AND HAS RECEIVED COUNTLESS
AWARDS OF RECOGNITION.

DR. PREUS BECAME PRESIDENT OF THE AMERICAN LUTHERAN CHURCH IN 1973
AND IS ALSO VICE PRES. OF THE LUTHERAN WORLD FEDERATION, A MEMBER OF
THE EXEC. COMMITTEE OF THE LUTHERAN COUNCIL IN THE U.S.A., AND A
MEMBER OF THE CENTRAL COMMITTEE OF THE WORLD COUNCIL OF CHURCHES.

GRANT'S
You Better Believe it!

PRINCE ROGER NELSON
WAS BORN IN MINNEAPOLIS.
HIS FATHER WAS A PIANIST
IN HIS OWN GROUP. ALAS
PRINCE WAS PLAYING THE
PIANO BY AGE SEVEN.

IN HIGH SCHOOL PRINCE PLAYED
BASKETBALL FOR CENTRAL.

HE HAS BEEN A WINNER OF
ALL CATEGORIES IN POP MUSIC
SURVEYS AND STARRED IN THE
MOTION PICTURES "PURPLE RAIN"
AND "UNDER THE CHERRY MOON."
AS A WARNER BROTHERS RECORDING
STAR AND LEADER OF THE BAND
"REVOLUTION," HE WON AN OSCAR FOR
BEST SONG SCORE WITH "PURPLE RAIN."

AL PAPAS Jr.

Prince

HIS ALBUMS "PARADE" AND "AROUND THE WORLD IN A DAY" WERE BEST
SELLERS. HE WAS CROWNED MUSIC WORLD'S KING BY WINNING ALL
THREE AWARDS: BEST SCORE, BEST ALBUM, AND BEST PERFORMANCE.

TO HELP THE AMERICAN NEEDY PRINCE'S "FOODBANK" PERFORMANCE
COLLECTED 23 TONS OF FOOD.

GRANT'S You Better Believe it!

WELL-KNOWN "60 MINUTES" TV CELEBRITY...

HARRY REASONER

... WAS A NATIVE-BORN IOWAN WHO MOVED TO MINNEAPOLIS AT AN EARLY AGE AND LATER ATTENDED WEST HIGH SCHOOL.

HIS FIRST JOB WAS AS A WRITER FOR THE NOW-DEFUNCT MINNEAPOLIS TIMES. SHORTLY THEREAFTER HE ENTERED THE SERVICE. UPON RETURNING HOME HE JOINED KEYD (NOW CHANNEL 9) AS A NEWS DIRECTOR. CBS NETWORK HIRED HIM IN 1956, AND BY 1965 HE HAD REPLACED DAN RATHER AS WHITE HOUSE NEWS CORRESPONDENT.

HIS VERY IN-DEPTH AND PERSONAL INTERVIEW OF GENERAL AND PRESIDENT DWIGHT D. EISENHOWER IS CONSIDERED A CLASSIC OF THIS GREAT AMERICAN.

HARRY MARRIED A LOCAL GIRL, KATHLEEN CARROLL, WHO BORE HIM SEVEN CHILDREN. REASONER HAS FOR THE PAST 15 YEARS RANKED AS ONE OF THE LEADING TV NEWS PERSONALITIES IN THE U.S.A., PARTICULARLY SINCE "60 MINUTES" WAS CREATED.

AL PAPAS Jr.

GRANT'S You Better Believe it!

WELL READ AND SOMETIMES CONTROVERSIAL COLUMNIST, DON RILEY, WAS BORN IN MINNEAPOLIS BUT HAS WRITTEN FOR THE ST. PAUL PRESS FOR 44 YEARS.

HE HAS AUTHORED BOOKS COVERING SALES, CRIMINOLOGY, ALCOHOLISM, AND FOOTBALL COACHING. HIS BOOK "HIGH AND DRY," ON ALCOHOLISM IS IN IT'S FOURTH PRINTING, AND WAS SYNDICATED IN 145 PAPERS BY THE NEW YORK TIMES. HIS "HOW TO EARN $50,000,000 IN SALES" AT AGE 28 WAS A PRENTICE-HALL BEST SELLER. STAGE RIGHTS TO HIS BOOK "THE GONIF" HAVE BEEN SOLD TO NEW YORK PRODUCERS.

DON HAS ALSO WRITTEN OVER 40 NATIONALLY-PUBLISHED MAGAZINE ARTICLES RANGING FROM IRISH WOLFHOUNDS, HARLEM GLOBETROTTERS, AND ARIZONA MOUNTAIN RANGES.

AS A NATIONALLY RENOWNED SPEAKER HE HAS COVERED TOPICS SUCH AS "SPORTS STORIES YOU'VE NEVER READ," AND "THE INSIDE LOOK AT AN ALCOHOLIC."

RILEY IS ON THE BOARD OF DIRECTORS OF "JUST SAY NO CLUBS" AND "TEAM HOUSE" COMBATING YOUTHFUL ADDICTION. CURRENTLY DON IS FINISHING TWO BOOKS: "JAMESTOWN 101" AND "ZARELDA-MOTHER OF JESSE JAMES."

Don Riley

GRANT'S You Better Believe it!

THE FAMED EDITOR AND AUTHOR WAS BORN IN MINNEAPOLIS WHERE HE GOT HIS LITERARY START BY WRITING A HISTORY OF WORLD WAR I WHEN NINE YEARS OLD.

HE GRADUATED FROM NORTH HIGH AT 16 AND THEN WENT TO THE U of M. HE PAID HIS TUITION BY WORKING FOR THE NOW-DEFUNCT MINNEAPOLIS JOURNAL.

AS EDITOR OF THE CAMPUS NEWS-PAPER HE WAS EXPELLED FROM SCHOOL FOR VIOLATING THE NO-SMOKING LAW. HIS INFRACTION GOT THE UNITED PRESS' ATTENTION, AND THEY HIRED HIM FOR THEIR ST. PAUL OFFICE. IT WAS HERE HE BECAME A GREAT ADMIRER OF J.J. HILL, WRITING REAMS ABOUT THE RAILROAD TYCOON.

AL PÃPAS Jr.

HARRISON SALISBURY

SALISBURY'S COVERAGE OF WORLD WAR II WAS ESPECIALLY THOROUGH WHEN RELAT-ING TO THE RUSSIANS WHOSE LANGUAGE AND CUSTOMS HE TOOK GREAT PAINS TO LEARN. MUCH LATER HE WROTE A 14 PART SERIES ON RUSSIA WHICH WON HIM THE 1955 PULITZER PRIZE.

LATER BECOMING AN EDITOR FOR THE NEW YORK TIMES, HE COVERED THE POLITICAL CONVENTIONS OF 1964 AND 1968, THE U.S. BOMBINGS OF HANOI, THE 75TH ANNIVERSARY OF THE BOLSHEVIK REVOLUTION, AND THE 1969 RUSSIAN-CHINESE WAR.

AFTER WRITING SEVERAL BOOKS WHICH WERE WELL RECEIVED, HE AND HIS WIFE HAVE NOW RETIRED TO A QUAINT VILLAGE IN CONNECTICUT WHERE HE STILL DOES SOME WRITING. HIS SISTER LIVES IN THE OLD FAMILY HOME IN KEN-WOOD, AND HE HAS OCCASIONALLY COMES BACK TO NOTE MINNEAPOLIS' PRO-GRESS WITH "AMAZEMENT."

GRANT'S You Better Believe it!

ERIC SEVAREID

...WAS BORN IN SOUTH DAKOTA, A SON OF A BANKER AND CITY COUNCIL-MAN. HIS HIGH SCHOOLING WAS AT MINNEAPOLIS CENTRAL WHERE HE WAS EDITOR OF THE SCHOOL NEWSPAPER.

WHILE ATTENDING THE 'U of M' HE WORKED FOR THE OLD MINNEAPOLIS JOURNAL. AFTER RECEIVING A B.A. DEGREE HE WENT TO PARIS TO WORK AS A CORRESPOND-ENT FOR THE N.Y. HERALD TRIBUNE.

IN 1939 ERIC WAS HIRED BY THE FAMED EDWARD R. MURROW FOR CBS.

SO, THIS IS WHAT ED MEANT BY THIS JOB BEING A DAY AT THE BEACH.

WELCOME TO ANZIO BEACH

DURING WORLD WAR II SEVAREID WAS THE FIRST TO BROADCAST FROM ANZIO BEACHEAD AND WAS AMONG THE FIRST TO ENTER ROME AND SOUTHERN FRANCE. LATER HE COVERED THE PEACE CONFERENCE IN SAN FRANCISCO.

HE WROTE A BOOK IN 1946 ENTITLED "NOT SO WILD A DREAM" WHICH IS STILL CONSIDERED A 'CULT FAVORITE' ON COLLEGE CAMPUSES.

GRANT'S You Better Believe it!

THIS GIANT OF COMIC STRIPS LEARNED HIS CARTOONING FROM A CORRESPONDENCE COURSE. HIS FATHER WAS A BARBER IN ST. PAUL WHERE CHARLES, NICKNAMED "SPARKY," ATTENDED CENTRAL HIGH.

Charles Schulz

DURING WW II HE WAS A STAFF SERGEANT LEADING A MACHINE GUN SQUAD. AFTER THE WAR HE WORKED FOR THE ST. PAUL PIONEER PRESS DISPATCH AND THE SATURDAY EVENING POST.

IN 1950 SCHULZ JOINED A CARTOON SYNDICATE STARTING WITH 8 NEWSPAPERS, THE MINNEAPOLIS STAR BEING ONE OF THEM. "PEANUTS" NOW APPEARS IN OVER 2,000 PAPERS THROUGHOUT THE WORLD AND IS THE MOST WIDELY SYNDICATED STRIP IN NEWSPAPER COMIC HISTORY. HIS LITTLE PALS HAVE MADE FEATURE LENGTH MOVIES, TV SPECIALS, A STAGE PRODUCTION AND HUNDREDS OF BOOKS. "HAPPINESS IS A WARM PUPPY" WAS A #1 SELLER IN 1963. HIS SNOOPY WAS A MASCOT IN THE APOLLO SPACE PROGRAM WHO WENT TO THE MOON. SCHULZ, HIMSELF, HAS BEEN A RECIPIENT OF THE "REUBEN," THE "OSCAR" OF CARTOONING.

A RELIGIOUS MAN, HE NEITHER DRINKS OR SMOKES.

FOR FUN HE OWNS AN ICE RINK WHERE HE PLAYS RIGHT WING IN A SENIOR HOCKEY LEAGUE.

AL PARAS JR.

GRANT'S
You
Better
Believe
it!

MAX SHULMAN WAS BORN IN
ST. PAUL WHERE HIS FATHER
WAS A HOUSE PAINTER. MAX
BEGAN WRITING AT FOUR
YEARS OLD.

IN HIGH SCHOOL HE WAS SO
"BUSY CHASING GIRLS AND
SHOOTING POOL" HE FLUNKED
OUT. ENTERING THE U of M
IN 1936 HE EDITED THE "SKI-
U-MAH MAGAZINE AND
WROTE FOR THE MINNESOTA
DAILY.

A YEAR AFTER GRADUATION
HE PUBLISHED HIS FIRST BOOK,
"BAREFOOT BOY WITH CHEEK."
THIS IS ONE OF THE ALL-TIME
CLASSICS OF COLLEGE HUMOR,
AND STILL SELLS WELL ON
CAMPUSES. THIS WAS FOLLOWED
BY "FEATHER MERCHANTS"
"ZEBRA DERBY" AND DOZENS
OF SHORT STORIES. HE LATER
COLLABORATED ON THE
"TENDER TRAP" AND WROTE
COLLEGE HUMOR FOR 200
COLLEGE NEWSPAPERS.

AL PAPAS Jr.

MAX SHULMAN

IN 1957 HE WROTE "RALLY ROUND THE FLAG BOYS" AND CBS HIRED HIM
TO WRITE A SERIES BASED ON "DOBIE GILLIS" THE TEENAGE HERO OF
MANY OF HIS SHORT STORIES.

GRANT'S *You Better Believe it!*

Ann Sothern

STAR OF STAGE-SCREEN AND TV WAS A MINNEAPOLIS NATIVE WHOSE REAL NAME WAS

Harriet Lake

HER PARENTS WERE IMPRESSED WITH LAKE HARRIET AND CHOSE TO NAME HER ACCORDINGLY!

SHE ATTENDED CENTRAL HIGH EXCELLING IN MUSIC, AND LATER REPRESENTED THE STATE OF MINNESOTA IN A NATIONAL CONTEST HELD IN DETROIT.

HER GREAT-GRANDFATHER, SIMON LAKE, WAS THE INVENTOR OF THE FIRST SUBMARINE "THE ARGONAUT."

HER ROLE AS "MAISIE" IN A MOVIE SERIES BROUGHT HER FAME. LATER SHE APPEARED ON TV IN "PRIVATE SECRETARY" AND "THE ANN SOTHERN SHOW."

You Better Believe it!

FORMER MINNESOTA "BOY-
WONDER" GOVERNOR, HAROLD
STASSEN WAS ELECTED AT AGE
31, AND DURING WORLD WAR II
WAS ADMIRAL "BULL" HALSEY'S
ASSISTANT.

HAROLD STASSEN

HE WAS INSTRUMENTAL IN THE FORMING OF THE UNITED NATION'S CHAR-
TER IN 1945, AND WAS ONE OF THE ORIGINAL SIGNERS. HE IS STILL
OFFERING HIS INPUT TOWARD THE UPDATING OF THAT DOCUMENT.

IN THE 1946 CLASSIC OF JOHN GUNTHER'S BOOK "INSIDE AMERICA," AN
ENTIRE CHAPTER WAS DEDICATED TO HIM, ENTITLED "STASSEN-YOUNG
MAN GOING SOMEWHERE."

SINCE THEN HE HAS GONE SEEKING PUBLIC OFFICE NATIONALLY, AND IN
BOTH PENNSYLVANIA AND MINNESOTA WITHOUT SUCCESS. IN 1948,
THOUGH, IT APPEARED THAT HE MIGHT BECOME THE REPUBLICAN CANDID-
ATE FOR PRESIDENT. A LATE SURGE BY DEWEY TOOK IT AWAY FROM
HIM. THERE ARE MANY HINDSIGHT SPECULATORS WHO BELIEVE HE WOULD
HAVE BEATEN HARRY TRUMAN AT THAT TIME.

STASSEN IS STILL ACTIVE IN POLITICS, RUNNING FOR THE U.S. CONGRESS
ON HIS ORIGINAL MINNESOTA TURF.

HONORARY CHAIRMAN OF MINNEAPOLIS HONEYWELL, THE WORLD LEADER IN CONTROL SYSTEMS AND COMPUTERS:

Harold W. Sweatt

HIS FATHER, WILLIAM R. SWEATT BECAME INTERESTED IN A SMALL FINANCIALLY TROUBLED FIRM CALLED ELECTRIC THERMOSTAT CO., WHICH HE RENAMED ELECTRIC HEAT REGULATOR CO.

GRANT'S You Better Believe it!

IN 1927 HAROLD HELPED HIS FATHER EFFECT A MERGER WITH HONEYWELL HEATING SPECIALTIES CO. OF WABASH, INDIANA. OUT OF THIS MARRIAGE HONEYWELL EVOLVED TO SPREAD IT'S ACTIVITY ALL OVER THE WORLD.

UNDER HAROLD SWEATT'S GUIDANCE THE COMPANY HAS BECOME THE WORLD'S LARGEST MANUFACTURER OF CONTROL SYSTEMS FOR HOMES, BUILDINGS, INDUSTRY, AND AEROSPACE IN ADDITION TO SYSTEMS AND CONTROLS FOR DEFENSE AND DATA PROCESSING EQUIPMENT.

FORTUNE MAGAZINE HAS DESCRIBED HAROLD SWEATT AS "ONE OF THE LEAST-KNOWN HEADS OF A FAMOUS SUCCESSFUL U.S. CORPORATION."

GRANT'S You Better Believe it!

AL PAPAS JR.

THIS MINNESOTA
VIKING QUARTERBACK
WAS THE FIRST ORIG-
INAL VIKING TO BE
ENSHRINED IN THE
PRO-FOOTBALL HALL
OF FAME.

Fran Tarkenton

OF THE TOTAL 18 SEASONS FRANCIS A. "FRAN" TARKENTON PLAYED
IN THE NFL, 13 OF THEM WERE WITH THE VIKINGS. HE COMPLET-
ED 3,686 PASSES FOR 342 TOUCHDOWNS, AND 47,003 YARDS.
HE ALSO RAN 674 TIMES FOR 3674 YARDS, MANY OF WHICH WERE
OF THE "SCRAMBLING FOR HIS LIFE" VARIETY. FRAN HAS BEEN
REFERRED TO AS "ONE OF THE GREATEST QUARTERBACKS TO EVER
PLAY THE GAME.

TARKENTON IS NOW CHAIRMAN OF THE BOARD OF BEHAVIORAL
SYSTEMS, INC., AND DOES BROADCAST WORK FOR NBC. RECENT-
LY HE EMERGED AS PART OF A NEW GROUP WHO MAY BE
ACQUIRING CONTROL OF THE MINNESOTA VIKINGS.

GRANT'S **You Better Believe it!**

HE WAS BORN AVROM HIRSH GOLDBOGEN IN NORTH MINNEAPOLIS.

AL PAPAS JR.

MIKE TODD

HIS FAMILY LATER MOVED TO BLOOMINGTON WHERE HIS PARENTS OPERATED A GENERAL STORE.

TODD BECAME ONE OF AMERICA'S GREATEST SHOWMEN AND PRODUCED THE JULES VERNE STORY "AROUND THE WORLD IN 80 DAYS." IT WON EVERY MAJOR AWARD.

HE ALSO DEVELOPED TODD AO CINEMATOGRAPHY FIRST USED IN ROGERS AND HAMMERSTEIN'S "OKLAHOMA".

AT THE TIME OF HIS DEATH IN A 1958 PLANE CRASH HE WAS MARRIED TO ACTRESS ELIZABETH TAYLOR.

MANY OF HIS IDEAS IN PROMOTING MOTION PICTURES AND EXHIBITION PROCEDURES HELPED CHANGE THE ENTIRE INDUSTRY.

Grant's You Better Believe it!

THE STAR OF "THE MAN FROM U.N.C.L.E." TELEVISION SERIES IS A FORMER RESIDENT OF MINNEAPOLIS WHO GRADUATED FROM NORTH HIGH SCHOOL IN 1950.

Robert Vaughn

TRAVELING!

TWEET

OF COURSE! IT'S BECAUSE I'M GOING PLACES...

WHILE AT NORTH HE WON LETTERS IN BASKETBALL AND TRACK. HE LATER STUDIED AT THE U of M ON AN ATHLETIC SCHOLARSHIP AND DID SPORTS REPORTING FOR THE MINNEAPOLIS STAR AND A LOCAL RADIO STATION. AN M.A. DEGREE CAME NEXT AT U.S.C.

SUCCESS CAME TO VAUGHN'S ACTING CAREER WHEN HE PLAYED A ONE-ARMED DRUNK IN "THE YOUNG PHILADELPHIANS" FOR WHICH HE WAS NOMINATED FOR BEST SUPPORTING ACTOR OF THE YEAR. HE ALSO CO-STARRED WITH YUL BRYNNER IN "THE MAGNIFICENT SEVEN."

NUMEROUS ROLES HAVE FOLLOWED HIM AS HAS INVOLVEMENT IN CALIFORNIA POLITICS. HE WAS ACTIVE IN HIS OPPOSITION TO THE VIETNAM WAR.

GRANT'S
You Better Believe it!

THIS PIONEER CIVIL RIGHTS LEADER WAS BORN IN ST. LOUIS. HE MOVED TO ST. PAUL AT AN EARLY AGE WHERE HE GREW UP AT 906 GALTIER STREET. AFTER GRADUATING FROM MECHANIC ARTS HE ATTENDED THE U of M WHERE HE WENT TO JOURNALISM SCHOOL. HE WROTE FOR THE MINNESOTA DAILY.

AL PAPAS Jr.

ROY WILKINS
1901-1981

WILKINS HELPED ESTABLISH ONE OF THE FIRST CHAPTERS OF THE N.A.A.C.P. IN ST. PAUL.

HE LATER ROSE TO GREAT PROMINENCE, NATIONALLY, BECOMING THE ASSOCIATION'S SPOKESMAN DURING SOME OF IT'S MOST CRITICAL PERIODS OF GROWTH. HIS SKILLFULL GUIDANCE WAS INSTRUMENTAL IN ACHIEVING SUCCESS IN PASSING LEGISLATION ELIMINATING MANY OF THE FORMER INJUSTICES INFLICTED ON BLACKS.

WILKIN'S RATIONALE AND PERSPECTIVES GAINED RESPECT FROM EVERY PRESIDENT SINCE HARRY TRUMAN AND HE HELPED TO AVOID POTENTIAL CRISES DURING THE HOT 60'S.

THE ST. PAUL ARENA WAS RENAMED AFTER WILKINS IN HIS HONOR.

GRANT'S You Better Believe it!

CHARLES "BUD" WILKINSON WAS BORN IN MINNEAPOLIS AND WENT TO WASHBURN HIGH SCHOOL.

HE ATTENDED THE U of M WHERE HE PLAYED GUARD AND QUARTERBACK ON BERNIE BIERMAN'S CHAMPION FOOTBALL TEAMS OF 1934, 1935, AND 1936.

BUD WILKINSON

AFTER SERVING IN THE NAVY DURING WORLD WAR II HE CAME HOME TO GO INTO BANKING. SOON HE WAS DIVERTED BACK TO FOOTBALL AND ENDED UP BECOMING HEAD COACH AT THE UNIVERSITY OF OKLAHOMA. HE REMAINED THERE 17 YEARS, DURING WHICH TIME HE HELD THE MOST SUCCESSFULL RECORD OF ANY ACTIVE COACH IN THE GAME. HE HAD AN OVER-ALL RECORD OF 145-29-4. HE HAD UNBEATEN STRINGS OF 31 AND 47 GAMES. HIS OKLAHOMA TEAMS ENJOYED FOUR UNDEFEATED SEASONS, SIX BOWL VICTORIES, AND THREE NATIONAL CHAMPIONSHIPS. IN 1969 BUD WAS NAMED TO THE NATIONAL FOOTBALL FOUNDATION'S HALL OF FAME.

IN 1961 PRESIDENT JOHN KENNEDY APPOINTED WILKINSON AS SPECIAL AID ON PHYSICAL FITNESS IN HIS CONCERN OVER AMERICAN YOUTH. LATER ON WILKINSON TOOK A BRIEF FLING AT PRO COACHING THE ST. LOUIS CARDINALS.

GRANT'S You Better Believe it!

THE NEW YORK YANKEES OUT-
FIELDER WAS BORN IN ST. PAUL.
WHILE ATTENDING THE U OF M
HE WAS A MULTI-TALENTED ATH-
LETE AND WAS LATER DRAFTED
BY THREE DIFFERENT PRO
SPORTS.

Dave Winfield

HE OPTED FOR BASEBALL WITH
SAN DIEGO AND SPENT EIGHT
YEARS WITH THAT ORGANIZATION.

AS A "FREE-AGENT" THE NEW
YORK YANKEES SIGNED HIM TO
WHAT HAS BEEN REFERRED TO AS
"THE MOST LUCRATIVE IN THE
HISTORY OF SPORTS."

WHILE STILL PERFORMING FOR THE
YANKEES, HE DEVOTES ALMOST AS
MUCH TIME TO THE DAVID M.
WINFIELD FOUNDATION, SERVING
UNDER-PRIVILEGED YOUTH.
DAVE IS ESPECIALLY PLEDGED TO
A "DRUG AWARENESS" PROGRAM
AIMED AT EDUCATING YOUNG-
STERS TO THE DANGERS OF
DRUG ABUSE, AND TEACHING
THEM TO SAY "NO."